Making a Movie

from concept to red carpet

Also by Dana Lustig

DIRECTOR

A Thousand Kisses Deep
Wild Cherry
Confessions of a Sociopathic Social Climber
Kill Me Later (story by)
Wedding Bell Blues (story by)

PRODUCER

Breakwater
Jungle
Look Away
The Frontier
Blackout (LA)
Her Name is Carla
Zoe
The Circle
Tough Luck

Heartbreak Hospital
Kill Me Later
Dancing in the Blue Iguana
Stranger Than Fiction
Black and White
Partners in Crime
Wedding Bell Blues
Power 98
Rave Review

CO-PRODUCER

Brick (Bergman Lustig Productions)

EXECUTIVE PRODUCER

Reading Lolita in Tehran
Checkout
Spider in the Web
Long Time Since

TV

Executive Producer 10 episodes
Very Important Man Season 2 (LA Season)

Executive Producer and Creator 10 episodes
The Americans – Docu Reality

Making a Movie

from concept to red carpet

Dana Lustig

Illustrations by Yuval Robichek-

SARSAPARILLA MEDIA
(sass•per•illa)

Los Angeles, CA

Text Copyright © 2025 by Dana Lustig
Illustrations Copyright © Yuval Robichek

Making a Movie: From Concept to Red Carpet

All rights reserved. No part of this book can be reproduced, transmitted, or stored in an information retrieval system in any form or by any means, graphic, electronic or mechanical including photocopying, taping and recording without prior written permission from Dana Lustig. For discounts on bulk sales, educational, corporate or promotional use please go to www.makingamoviebook.com

First edition 2025

Library of Congress Cataloging-in-Publication Data

For permission to reproduce contact
Permissions, Dana Lustig Productions

Book Designer: Diana Wilburn
Editor: Annette Goliti Guitierrez
Editor: Samantha Silvay
Legal Advisor: Ben Reder

Primary Typeface: New Zen

Hardback ISBN: 979-8-9915134-0-1
Paperback ISBN: 979-8-9915134-1-8
E-book: 979-8-9915134-2-5

Printed In the United States of America

www.makingamoviebook.com
or
www.danalustig.com

10 9 8 7 6 5 4 3 2 1

For the entrepreneur wanting to invest in a movie, for the film school graduate who wants to make their first movie, and for anyone who has been dreaming of bringing their great ideas to life, this book is your road map to the journey and a call to action.

This book is also for the moms and dads who can't figure out what their kids are doing when they claim to be filmmakers.

"If I am here, it is because people love the movie, so it is always a question of love."

-Roberto Benigni, Oscar Speech

About This Book

I wrote this handbook to encourage anyone who wants to take the plunge and make an indie movie. Today, especially, there are no excuses; if you have the devotion, tenacity, and most importantly, a great story to tell, you can do it. This book can serve as a practical roadmap, a condensed checklist of the entire process of making an indie film.

Each of the separate steps in the process could be the subject of extended research and study. However, in my attempt to identify the steps a filmmaker will encounter along the way, I tried to limit myself to one page per subject in order to keep it a concise, fast and cohesive read.

This book is told through my lens as a director, producer and storyteller, straight from the trenches. Based on my own experiences, I've learned that whether you make your first movie for fifty thousand dollars, three million dollars or even for twelve million dollars, the same fundamentals apply to any budget.

However, making a movie is not only about the checklist, which anyone can figure out. It's about the glue that holds it all together—love, passion, determination, and the commitment to tell a story. Therefore, I have added anecdotes from my personal journey as a filmmaker, mostly stories about perseverance and overcoming challenges with the resilience born of a strong sense that filmmaking is my life's calling.

Throughout my career, I have worked with many first-time directors, writers, producers, and financiers, and I realized that the information I take for granted as a professional is not widely known. For some, the process of making a movie can be daunting. So I developed a lecture series to give an overview of the entire evolution—from concept to the release of the movie. I truly believe that no matter your role in the film business, you should zoom out, see the full picture, and be aware of what each department does.

So here are the highlights of my lectures, covering explanations of many of the terms and definitions used in the jargon of the indie filmmaking business.

Every movie is unique in how it has come about, been written, financed, filmed, and distributed, and each brings a whole new set of surprises, challenges, and sometimes unimaginable happy accidents.

So if and when you fly to Colombia to film a scene on a river but the river is dry, or the star's fancy costume is locked in a local store and your actor is on the verge of a nervous breakdown, or when an actor kicks a first-time director off the set, or when your stunt performer is swept away in raging waters, you'll need to find fast and creative solutions. There is no "problem solving" school, however, if you prep right, and follow the basics covered in the book, when troubles come, and they will, you will be able to face them with confidence, and will be prepared to find fast, safe and constructive solutions.

In putting this book together I have been reminded how much I love making movies and meeting others who share my passion.

Contents

Introduction

Disclaimer

Parts

1 **Content is King**

2 **Financing**

3 **Preproduction**

4 **Finally Filming**

5 **Postproduction**

6 **Distribution & Marketing**

7 **Encore**

Acknowledgments

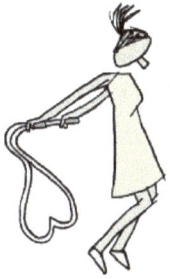

Introduction

When I was ten years old, two major things happened in my life: my parents divorced and I became a storyteller. As my family fell apart, I was flooded with thoughts and wonders about the world and its meaning. The tool I used instinctively to make sense of everything was telling stories to myself and others. I started to dramatize my life and with my sister Nadine built a puppet theater in our driveway and told stories to whoever agreed to listen. Little did I know then that this would become my lifelong passion and occupation.

I was twelve when my grandmother took me to Europe for my bat mitzvah. In Zurich, Switzerland, she bought me a ticket for a matinee to watch *Heidi*. The theater was empty, and the movie was dubbed into Swiss German, which I didn't understand. But I got the gist of it, and I was transfixed. I was spellbound by the breathtaking scenery, the stunning cinematography, and the orchestral score. I became immersed in the love story, the feeling of longing, and the themes of faith, poverty, and a little girl in search of a home. I was inspired by the belief that we can all overcome hardship and adversity with love, faith, and support, and I fully experienced the power of cinema.

I stepped onto a real movie set for the first time at age sixteen when I was walking back from an ice-skating class, and that was it. My imagination was captivated. I saw it from afar—a huge biblical, colorful ancient market with hundreds of extras roaming around in costumes, big lamps, a tall crane with a camera on it, tons of trucks, and an American and Israeli crew working in harmony, creating a make-believe world. I stood there mesmerized.

I didn't know who was who on the set. This tall American guy was using a megaphone to give directions. I thought he was the director, but I later found out that the quiet, heavy-set man sitting by his side was the director. He would get up and speak quietly with the actors, and the loud guy was the assistant director.

I discreetly walked about the camp, awed by the props truck, the production design, the camera, the makeup artist's huge trailer with the string of lights around the mirrors, and the huge fake walls of the old city of Jerusalem. Weirdly, I felt at home; I felt that this was where I wanted to be. I had found my village.

I loved seeing all those professionals from the different departments working together in harmony to tell the same story. I gained courage and approached someone who seemed important, and asked if I could get a job. He introduced me to the "water girl" and asked her to train me.

In Israel, it gets so hot that one person on set has the sole job of handing out water to the cast and crew. So I learned when was a good time to serve, how to get onto the set without interrupting a shot, and how to fill twenty-four cups of water and carry them without tripping. But more importantly, I got a chance to observe how a movie was made while getting to be a part of the magic.

So began my love affair with cinema and the art of storytelling. But how do you take a passion for something and make it a reality? Where do you start?

I knew I needed to learn everything I could about the art and business of film-making if I was going to make this dream a reality, so I took acting classes. Then during my army service (Israel requires military service for everyone, both male and female), I performed in the army theater and studied video production. Those experiences helped me find work in the industry once I was released, mainly as a video editor and a production manager on documentaries and commercials. And then, being young, curious, and ambitious, I decided to take a chance and try my luck in the United States. I first landed in New York, and being so naïve, I walked into CBS studios on 42nd street, asking for a job. While all my friends were still working in the falafel stand, I got a job as an editor for CBS Morning Business News even though I hardly spoke English and didn't know anything about business.

This was great, but I wanted more. I moved to Miami and worked for a year on cruise ships, directing and editing videos of the ships and islands to be sold to the passengers. After lots of fun in the sun the time came when I figured I needed to study filmmaking in depth. I heard of a film school, which was run by a "working faculty" with a focus on teaching by making movies. I knew this was the right place for me, so I applied to the American Film Institute (AFI). As a very selective school, the chances were slim, but I didn't leave myself any other choice. I had to get in.

I didn't apply anywhere else, and I flew in for an interview with the dean, Jean Firstenberg, whose encouraging manner I will always cherish. I was accepted! But then it dawned on me that I couldn't afford AFI along with the living expenses, and as a foreigner, I couldn't get financial aid or a loan. But I have this habit of diving in first, taking the plunge, and then figuring it out—a trait that has served me well in this business and in life.

Then my grandfather called me. He was a Holocaust survivor, and as a Jew in Europe, he suffered an incredible amount of humiliation and antisemitism at university, even before the war. So when he heard that I had gotten into a prestigious educational institution, he took the money he had just received from the German government as retribution to allow me to go to school.

His belief in me was motivating. At AFI, we were supposed to produce three short movies during the first year. I did four. I was the first on campus in the morning. Even after wild nights at Borders in Hollywood, I would wake up and rush over to campus, yearning to learn. I met new friends for life, and we would passionately fight for our vision while challenging each other and learning from our legendary professors. This complete immersion in the art of filmmaking was the foundation of my film career.

For a class at AFI, I came up with an idea for a script, *Kill Me Later*, about a young woman who was contemplating suicide, and I decided to produce it as a short after

I graduated. I would star in it, and I convinced my talented classmates, Annette Goliti Gutierrez and Maria Ripoll, the ingenious Spanish director, to write with us and direct it.

To finance the short, Maria and I put a small desk in the parking lot of Gelson's supermarket on Franklin Avenue. This was our early version of crowdfunding. We wrangled a crew for free and the roof of a storage building for our location. I loved every moment of it except, a day before the shoot, Maria and I went to the fanciest salon in Beverly Hills for my haircut—not the right move to experiment with an extreme makeover the day before production...don't do it. They cut it short and I couldn't stand it, but I guess it didn't bother anyone else, and we went on to win the audience award at the acclaimed short film festival in Oberhausen, Germany.

While working as the production manager on a movie produced by my friend Yoram Barzilai, and directed by the talented Rob Spera, both AFI alums, I met Ram Bergman. Like me, he was a young dreamer from Israel who came to Hollywood to become a film producer. He was smart, ambitious, craving to learn, and had no ego. We both worked hard on that production, and at night, when I was wrapping and closing the set, he always stayed to help. We would carry out the garbage bags and make sure that all the lights were off, doors locked, and the place was ready for the next day's shoot.

Then we would sit in his funny convertible—which later was towed, never to be seen again—and dream about the movies we would like to make. It was the beginning of a great partnership, and we decided to open our own production company and start making movies. We printed business cards with the name Bergman Lustig Productions and off we went.

Ram and I produced many films together over the next few years, but of course I was most excited about my directorial debut, *Wedding Bell Blues*. So all those jobs I had done—from water girl and extra, to grip, PA, editor, production manager, being a videographer on cruise ships and then the film school experience—all prepared me for the big moment when I got to the first day on set as a director.

I remember the multi-talented supermodel, author, and a wonderful actress, Paulina Porizkova, who was one of the stars of the movie, asking me on the first day of shooting by the craft service table, "How do you feel?" And I told her, "Home."

So whether you decide to take the plunge after reading this book or not, I hope you'll keep enjoying and going to the movies.

Disclaimer

I am not a lawyer, and I do not attempt to provide any legal advice. I am simply sharing insights from my own experience of reading, commenting on, and signing hundreds of contracts throughout my career. My goal is to shed light on the things you might want to consider when negotiating your own deal or handling the many deals and legal documents involved in making a movie.

You should always hire a professional entertainment lawyer to provide you with proper advice and to draft and negotiate your contracts.

PART ONE
CONTENT IS KING

Don't Shoot for The Sky Without Bullets

The Magic Words: Intellectual Property

Original Script and Spec Script

Book Adaptation

Life Rights

Adaptation from Short Movies

Articles, Remakes and All the Rest

Public Domain

It's a Matter of the Heart

Securing Rights

Option Agreement

Shopping Agreement

Purchase Agreement and Exercising of Option

Writing Agreement

Development Funds

Securing Rights by Partnerships

Chain of Title

Errors and Omissions Insurance

Pitching

Pitch Meeting

Pitch Deck

Sizzle Reel

Sharing Your Original Ideas

Start the Buzzzzzz

Be in the Know

"Don't Shoot for the Sky Without Bullets"

When I graduated from AFI, I was full of energy and ambition, eager to start working in the industry. Having relocated to the United States just two years prior, I retained that Israeli mindset, believing that everyone was merely one degree of separation away. I could reach anyone I wished to connect with.

Using my tenacity, I managed to schedule a meeting with a high-profile producer. The meeting went great. The producer showed interest in my journey, including my military service and educational background, and eventually he posed the pivotal question, "What do you aspire to do?"

To this I promptly replied, "I want to produce and direct films."

He then said, "Excellent, do you have any material to share? Perhaps a script you'd like to produce?"

Then it dawned on me... I had nothing, and red-faced I replied, "No, I don't."

The esteemed producer smiled and then imparted the most invaluable advice I've ever received...

"Honey, don't shoot for the sky without bullets."

That counsel, though delivered in a somewhat old-fashioned way, remains forever in my consciousness. Subsequently, I embarked on my lifelong journey to seek out and develop interesting and worthy content—original scripts, books, articles, true stories, and stories derived from my own life.

As a producer this is your main job...find the bullets!

The Magic Words: Intellectual Property

Everyone wants to base their project on intellectual property or IP that has the potential to gain public interest. If you send a cold email to any executive in town, and the subject says, "Based on a NYT best seller," or "Based on an incredible true story of survival featured on CNN," or "a remake of a successful foreign movie," or "a script based on a short film that won the audience award in Tribeca," or any other interesting IP, you are almost guaranteed to receive a reply, at least from an assistant to the executive. But make sure you own the rights to whatever you're pitching, or you risk looking very unprofessional in the short run and possibly even being sued in the long run.

Intellectual Property can be derived from:

- an original script
- a book or short story
- true events in which you obtain the life rights for the real people
- a story based on a published article
- a blog, vlog or podcast
- a short movie
- a remake of a foreign language movie or an older movie
- games
- plays

Original Script and Spec Script

While any script can be based on IP, an original script under copyright law is one created solely from the author's imagination rather than taken from someone else's copyrighted work. Whether a story is from the fruit of your imagination, based on your own experience, or inspired by a location you visited, people you met, a song you heard, or anything else that got you motivated, the more specific the idea and the writing is, the more relatable the story will be. Trust your instincts, and don't look for a generic story. Embrace a particular, different, innovative, quirky vision to tell a universal story.

An original script can be written on spec, or someone can be hired to write one. The term "spec" script comes from the word speculation as it is written without a guarantee that the movie will be produced; however, the writer working on their own spec script, will own all rights to it. This means they will be able to negotiate terms of engagement once a producer commits to make the movie.

If a screenwriter is hired to write a script, it will usually be "work for hire," and the person who paid for it will obtain most of the rights.

You may also get lucky and read a wonderful spec script written by a novice writer that's sitting in their drawer, in which case you can try to get the rights from them, so you can pitch their script and try to set it up. In that case you will agree on a proper compensation to be paid later when financing for the movie is secured.

As with any financial negotiations, it is always wise to speak with an entertainment lawyer before agreeing to any specific deals.

❀ *Most of the movies I have produced and/or directed were based on original spec scripts. The first movie I directed was Wedding Bell Blues. The idea was sparked upon my return from my younger brother's wedding in Israel, where everyone was feeling sorry for me for still being single. It was humiliating.*

I decided right then to go to Vegas with a friend, any friend, marry them, and then immediately divorce them. Being thirty and divorced seemed less pathetic to me back then than being thirty and single. While this crazy plan was going through my head, I started dating a drummer, who would later become my husband. Naturally I called off the plan, but then I thought, wouldn't this be a great idea for a movie? So I contacted my writer friend Annette, who according to her Armenian family, like me, was also apparently a spinster at twenty-nine. People loved the idea, and we were able to engage interest in the script.

Book Adaptation

Production companies and financiers frequently seek to acquire rights to bestselling books, anticipating that readers will be interested in seeing the story adapted to film. While rights to popular books can be expensive, there are opportunities to obtain rights to lesser-known works with untapped potential, like older bestsellers or foreign language books. When securing the rights to a book, it's important to discuss your plans for adaptation with the author and determine whether they will agree to changes and dramatization of parts of the story.

❀ The first book adaptation I directed was based on the NYT bestseller Confessions of a Sociopathic Social Climber. The movie was a success, and I was inspired to find another book to adapt. Upon my return home from filming, I approached Yossi Ghinsberg, the author of one of my favorite books, Jungle. Over lunch when I asked to option the book rights, Yossi politely rejected my offer. He wanted a big company, perhaps a studio, to make a movie.

Knowing that Yossi was leaving LA in a couple of hours, I dejectedly drove home, having missed my chance. Then, suddenly, I stopped driving. With renewed determination, I called Yossi and told him I was coming over, and all I needed was two minutes of his time. He reluctantly agreed, and excited for my second chance, I sped back to convince him. I was pulled over by a policeman and received a five hundred dollar speeding ticket, but I arrived just as Yossi was carrying his suitcase to a waiting taxi. I looked into his eyes and told him, "Yossi, I promise you, I will make your movie. It will be my mission, and I will protect and stay true to the spirit of the story and the integrity of the people portrayed." After years of development with other producers who had changed the essence of the story and tried to make it an action movie rather than a deeply spiritual survival story, he took a moment to assess whether I was genuine. Finally, he shook my hand in agreement.

Life Rights

When you want to write a story about a true event that involves people who are living, it is often necessary to purchase the "life rights" from those people. This will give you an advantage over anyone else who wants to tell the same story, and production companies prefer projects that come with life rights. Very importantly, obtaining life rights also protects you against lawsuits, and may be required by an errors and omissions insurance company before it issues your production an E&O insurance policy.

❀ *Years ago, I pitched a TV show called The Medium to Viacom. My idea was to make a show about a medium who helps solve mysteries by connecting with dead people. The executives at Viacom loved the idea, but they did not pick it up. A few months later, I read in the trades that CBS/Viacom was developing a show called Medium, and the idea sounded almost identical to mine. Outraged, I called my then-agent, ready to sue. He counseled that for many reasons, I should let it go, but mainly because the main character on their show was based on a real-life medium from Texas with whom they were collaborating. I was heartbroken, but the life rights they had acquired prohibited me from doing anything about it.*

Adaptation from Short Movies

Sometimes, a short film has such a great concept that developing it into a feature is merited. Such adaptations are most frequently made from successful or award-winning student or indie productions. Taking a well-executed short and turning it into a full-length feature is no easy task, but there are wonderful examples of it being done successfully, such as *Whiplash* and *Lights Out*.

"The Miracle of Love"

❈ *I came up with the idea for Kill Me Later while listening to "The Miracle of Love" by Eurythmics, which lyrics talk about the healing power of love, and decided to turn my idea into a short film. Since my younger sister's tragic death at twenty, I have often been drawn to themes of survival, the search for hope and the power of love to heal. After the success of the short film, Annette and I decided to adapt the short script into a feature length movie. Extending the plot, was a big undertaking. We retained the core of the story: a woman standing on a roof preparing to jump to her death is taken hostage by a bank robber. He offers her a deal: "Be my hostage now, and I'll kill you later." Through their journey together, she finds a reason to live.*

In the short version, the robber is killed at the end of the movie. In the feature, however, they jump together off a bridge, escape the authorities and then go off to live on a magical island. The wonderful Selma Blair and Max Beesley starred in the film, which had a very different vibe and style from the short, but the core idea and the main scene on the roof remained very much the same.

Articles, Remakes and All the Rest

Published Articles

Investigative reporters are "in". Many great films are based on published articles. Although some of these stories may be in the public domain, it is wise to secure the article rights from the writer or publisher. While it may be prohibitively expensive to obtain rights from leading publications, just like with books, an ocean of untapped material remains in local newspapers and foreign publications. Some investigative reporters are happy to collaborate in order to bring their story to the screen.

Remakes

You can obtain rights to remake foreign films into English speaking ones or vice versa. You can also remake older movies and bring a fresh perspective to timeless stories. To do this, you need to obtain the rights to the original films from the filmmaker or distributors (or both) who control them. *A Star Is Born* has been made four times already in English, and the French megahit *The Intouchables* was remade into the successful movie *The Upside*.

Podcasts, Blogs, Vlogs, Games and Social Media

Current storytelling mediums such as podcasts and blogs are also rich sources of content. Again, you have to obtain the rights from the original creator. For example, the 2015 Twitter thread "Zola" became an award-winning movie in 2020. Many companies with development funds are looking to develop content and can pay big bucks to acquire properties. It is hard to compete with these companies, so look for the little gems that you can shepherd without spending a huge amount on development.

Public Domain

Movies and TV shows are often based on material that is in the public domain. Any such material can be used freely without the need of clearing rights. Generally, works enter the public domain seventy years after the death of author if the work was created after January 1978. Most works created before then will go into the public domain ninety-five years after publication, as will any owned by a company based on material that was authored as work for hire.

January 1 is known as Public Domain Day as a list of content that has newly fallen into the public domain is announced. If your story is based on public domain material, anyone else could be working on the same story. Therefore, you must bring your unique perspective so your project shines and stands out from similar projects.

Contemporary stories about living people can also be in the public domain as long as they have been published widely. However, you must be extra vigilant about not defaming anyone as you might be exposed to a lawsuit. Defamation is the action of damaging the good reputation of someone. For this reason, names are often changed and disclaimers are written. It is helpful if the character in your film cannot be readily identified as a specific real person. Change their gender, their hair color, and give them stinky feet…no one will come forward to sue you. Who wants to admit they have stinky feet? But again, talk with your lawyer.

❀ *Years ago, while working on cruise ships, I developed a fascination with pirates. So with a very talented young writer, Marianne Wibberley, we developed a story about Mary Read, a brave and ferocious seventeenth-century female pirate who masqueraded as a man. Then we found out that Renny Harlin was making a movie about a female pirate, and we sadly put our hard work in a drawer. Maybe one day we'll revisit it. I think we should … Marianne?*

It's a Matter of the Heart

For me, the reason to commit to a project begins with love—an irresistible connection to the story. It's that spark of creative excitement: fascination, curiosity, and enthusiasm about the plot, the characters, their arcs, and the overarching theme. Sometimes it's a feeling without a clear reason, a deep need to tell that story. Committing to a project feels like jumping into a long-term relationship, full of ups and downs, but that passion sustains me through the entire roller coaster ride, no matter the outcome.

You should consider many factors before committing to a project in the film industry, and the decision should never be made lightly. Developing a project can take years, with no guarantee the movie will be made.

So, beyond my initial instinct, I focus on three key elements:

The Story:
While the plot, backdrop, era, genre, and location are easy to identify, I'm most interested in understanding the deeper layers of the story. What is the theme? What moral dilemmas do the characters face? How interesting are the main characters, and what are their flaws and virtues? What are their external goals, and what are their deep internal needs? Do they have an arc?

I also ask myself: Why should I tell this story? Why now? How is it relevant? Who is the audience? Will the script attract a great cast? These are just a few of the questions I consider. In developing a script, I pay close attention to the choices characters make, especially the crucial decisions toward the end of the film. Are these choices different from those made at the start of the movie?

As Academy Award-winning writer Waldo Salt said, "Near the movie's end, the main character confronts a tough choice with a high cost." If there's no cost, the decision lacks weight. The moment when the character's decisions reveal the price they're willing to pay, defines what truly matters to them and encapsulates their overall journey. These moral and ethical questions are often the reason I commit to a project.

The Reality:
I estimate roughly the budget that would be required based on various factors: Is it contemporary, period, or futuristic? How many characters and locations are involved? Is it a small, intimate drama or a large-scale action movie with stunts and special effects? These considerations help me assess whether it's realistic for me to be able to put the financing together for the project or is too far-fetched for me to get involved.

The Team:
Another crucial element is the team. I thrive when working with people I trust and respect, knowing we'll spend years together making the film. A supportive, honest, and well-meaning team is priceless. Filmmaking is collaborative, but it's also demanding as we navigate different opinions, egos, and visions. Trust, integrity, and commitment make all the difference, especially in high-stress situations. Knowing that your team has your back is essential as you work through challenges together.

When I commit to a project, I hope it will be a gratifying experience. Regardless of how many "no's" I might face, I need to believe in the project enough to keep going and find new ways to make it happen.

In the end, the question I ask myself is: Will developing this project over the next few years inspire me? Will I learn something about the world and myself in the process?

Securing Rights

Once you fall in love with a script, book, story, article, or any other piece of IP, and you are committed to putting an endless amount of energy into bringing it to the screen, you'll need to secure the rights to the property. This has to be done prior to pitching the project anywhere in town, or you might put yourself in a very embarrassing situation if someone likes your project and you do not have the rights for it.

Here are the different agreements types to consider:

- **Option Agreement:** a contract between a writer or rights holder and a producer that gives the producer exclusive rights to develop and purchase the material. The producer will pay a fee to the rights owner for these rights for a limited agreed time. However, the producer will not be obligated to purchase the rights until the movie is financed and goes into production.

- **Shopping Agreement:** a short agreement that gives the producer the exclusive rights to shop the source material around town. Terms are left to be negotiated in good faith when the producer can secure financing.

- **Purchase Agreement:** Rights Acquisition Agreement—the final purchase of the material, which you have optioned, in perpetuity.

- **Writing Agreement:** You can hire a writer for an agreed upon fee to write a script, a synopsis based on your original idea, or an adaptation from underlined material. These services will be considered "work for hire," and the producer who is paying for the writing services will own all rights.

An entertainment lawyer will handle the drafting of any of these options. The terms for each one of the above agreements vary depending on whether you option a written script, a book, life rights, an article, or any other underline material.

Option Agreement

The main points to be negotiated between the owner of the material and a producer in an option agreement are as follows:

- **Duration:** How long the agreement will be binding—customarily anywhere between six months to five years. It is crucial to have enough time, especially if the script is not yet written, such as when optioning book rights. It may take years before you have a script that can be shopped in the market.

- **Reasonable Option Fee:** Agreed fee for the option. (Even if you receive the option for no fee, you should pay at least one dollar.)

- **Purchase Price and Exercise of Option:** The final fixed purchase price of the material should be stated in the option agreement. When the movie is financed and goes into production, the IP needs to be purchased in perpetuity, and the rights will be transferred to the production entity. Often, as the budget of the movie may be unknown when you first option the material the purchase price is calculated as a percentage of the final budget with a minimum fee guaranteed as well as a maximum, "a floor and ceiling." A customary fee for a script would be two to three percent of the budget of the movie. There may be exclusions from the budget, which won't be included in calculating the fee.

- **Extending the Option:** The right to extend the option agreement for a certain fee, usually an annual fee will be negotiated.

- **Credits:** Such as story by, screenplay by, based on a book by, based on an idea by, based on an article by, etc. Sometimes writers will need to share the writing credits if more than one writer was involved or if another writer was hired to do a rewrite.

- **Fees for Rewrites:** Define how many drafts the writer will be obligated to perform, for what fee, and the fee for additional drafts. Usually, the producer is not obligated to hire the writer for those rewrites but will have the option to do so under the agreement. Usually, the producer will ask for all the above fees to be applicable against the final purchase price of the material, and the work done will be considered as "work for hire." This means that whoever paid for the re-write, will own the rights for them. But beware, if the option to the underlined material, i.e. the original script, book, article or life rights which the rewrites are based off, has expired, than the rewrites cannot be used even if they are paid for in full .

- **Rewrites by Other Writers:** The agreement will state whether the producer has the rights to hire other writers to perform subsequent rewrites. This is standard in most option agreements.

- **Contingent Compensation and Backend:** Points, profit participation and/or bonus payments will be part of the agreement. Oftentimes the writer will receive about two and a half percent of the net profits. Bonuses for sole credit or a huge sale will also be negotiated.

- **Subsequent Productions:** Remakes, sequels, or spinoff rights.

- **Union Script Status:** If you're working with a writer who is a member of the WGA or any other writer's union, the production company will become signatory to the union and abide to its negotiated terms in regards to fees, credit, residuals, etc.

- **Invitations:** Invite the writer to visit the set for a certain number of days with paid flights and accommodation, as well as to the premiere of the movie or the first festival screening.

Shopping Agreement

A shopping agreement is a simpler and shorter document than an option agreement. It offers you the exclusive right to "shop" or pitch the material without paying to option it. Usually, a shopping agreement states that if you find someone who wants to make a movie based on the property, the owner of the property will negotiate for the sale of the property in good faith. It is important to add that the terms and final purchase price to be negotiated must be customary within the standards of the business. You have to make sure that the agreement guarantees that you will be attached to the project as a producer or director upon terms that you will negotiate yourself. The shopping agreement should say that the owner of the IP can't sell the property unless you are reasonably satisfied with your deal.

Purchase Agreement and Exercising of Option

Prior to commencing principal photography of the movie, the producer must purchase the IP. This will usually happen when the movie is about to close financing. At that point, the producer will "exercise the option," meaning that the lawyer will have the writer or rights holder, upon payment from the producer, acknowledge in writing that they have received the payment and the rights to the material are transferred to the production company.

This needs to happen prior to the expiration of the option agreement.

The same process applies to a shopping agreement. The difference is that a final price for the IP will be negotiated with the producer/financier at the time of purchase.

If you have the financial backing and feel confident that you will be able to raise financing to make the movie, you can purchase the IP outright instead of optioning it.

If the agreement is subject to the Writers Guild of America (i.e., the writer is a member of the WGA) or any other writer's union around the world, the writer retains certain rights to the property, including the right to receive residuals and other compensations.

Writing Agreement

When a producer or director hires a writer to write a script, a story, a pitch deck, an outline, or any other type of work, the parties sign a writer's agreement, which will most often be categorized as a work for hire agreement. This means that as long as the writer is paid in full, they do not control or own any rights to the property. The rights to the written material will be owned in full by the person who hired the writer.

The writer's agreement will address many of the same points that are covered in the option agreement such as screen credit, fees and payments, how many rewrites and polishes of the script are expected and for what kind of fees, who will write the sequels and/or adaptations, the option to hire additional writers for rewrites if needed, profit participation and bonuses, invitations to festivals and premiere, and more.

As the writing will often be done prior to any guarantees that the movie will be filmed, a fee for writing will be negotiated, and then another final fixed price will be negotiated to be paid if and when the movie is shot. This amount will be calculated as a percentage from the budget with a floor and a ceiling.

The fees that will be paid during the writing period will, in most cases, be applicable against the final purchase price of the script when the movie goes into production. For instance, all fees that were paid during the writing period will be deducted from the final purchase price.

If the writer is a member of any of the writer's guilds, the contract must abide by union rules. There are different payment and fee tiers to accommodate for the different budget level of projects.

Development Funds

Unless you have your own funds to spend on development, you may need to raise what we call "development funds" in order to progress with your project. You might need to pay for option rights for the IP, create pitch materials, or hire a casting director and attorney. You may need the funds to fly for preliminary scouts and meetings. Development funds are not easy to come by. They are the riskiest type of film investment because there is no guarantee that the movie being developed will ever happen. However, the amount required to fund development is much smaller than the amount needed to finance the actual production of a film.

Investors in the development of a film are usually accorded an executive producer credit and a promise that the investment will be repaid with interest from the budget of the movie upon the financing but, no later than the commencement of principal photography. This is different than an equity investor in the movie, who will receive their investment back from future revenues the movie generates. The development investor will also receive a couple of negotiated points from the net profits.

❄ *Once I secured the rights for the book* Jungle, *I pitched it all over town to major production companies. Everyone loved the story but told me to come back when I had a fully developed script. The book was not enough for anyone to commit. One Shabbat dinner with my good friends Jay Zohar and Michal Rapaport, I casually mentioned the book and my intention to turn it into a movie. Little did I know, they were great admirers of it, and as patrons of the arts, they asked how they could support my efforts. I told them I was looking for development funds and they committed right then and there. I told them this was a high-risk investment, but they insisted. With the funds, I was able to secure a lawyer, fly to Australia, and bring on acclaimed writer Justin Monjo to write the script.*

Securing Rights by Partnerships

Developing and getting a project financed and ready to film can take many years. Unless one has unlimited financial resources, repeatedly optioning material can get expensive. This puts one at risk of losing the rights to a project where time, energy, and funds have been invested. In these cases, forming a partnership with the IP holder or writer can be an attractive option for both sides. For the producer, partnering with the writer allows more time to develop the material and secure financing.

Under a partnership agreement the rights holder may have more input in the development process, and will usually be awarded an executive producer credit. An equal partnership—pooling all producing, writing, and sometimes directing fees into one shared pool—can also work well. I've done this a few times myself, and it builds trust among all parties. It ensures that everyone has each other's best interests at heart when negotiating fees and profit participation with financiers.

❋ *When I first started the negotiations with Yossi Ghinsberg to obtain the rights to* Jungle, *he wanted a renewable option fee for each year I held the rights. I knew it would take me a while to develop the project (it eventually took twelve), so I could not afford those fees. Therefore, I proposed that we become equal partners, splitting evenly anything I made as a producer and anything I could negotiate for the book rights.*

This partnership allowed me the time I needed to raise development funds, find a screenwriter, and work on more than ten drafts until, eventually, we obtained a deal with Arclight Films, and the film was greenlit. During all this time, Yossi knew I had his back in negotiations due to our status as equal partners.

On Wedding Bell Blues *and* Kill Me Later, *Ram, Annette, and I had a similar deal. We all became equal partners in the projects, and Annette wrote numerous drafts on spec for no fee, trusting that we would be able to make the movies, which we did.*

Chain of Title

One of the first things any financier or production company who might be interested in your project will ask is whether you have a clear chain of title (COT). This documentation proves that you have the right to produce the project—that all necessary rights to the intellectual property (IP) are clear and that all contracts and deals are signed. In such a case, there won't be any issue with third parties who may make a claim once you go into production or release the movie.

Chain of title can be long and complicated, especially in cases of projects that are being remade or were previously optioned or developed by other filmmakers. In those cases, again, all contracts are part of the COT and need to be reviewed by an entertainment lawyer. It is, therefore, important that you keep track of all legal documents related to your IP, including all e-mail correspondence.

Note: If a third-party producer previously tried unsuccessfully to make the project, development fees may be attached. These are the monies that producers spent trying to put together the project. These monies may include fees paid to writers, the costs of scouting, casting directors, and even the producer's overhead. Often, these fees need to be repaid to the previous producer before you can clear the title.

❀ *The book* Jungle *was written in 1982. Since then, it had been optioned a few times by notable producers. Those options had expired and the rights to the book reverted to Yossi, including rights from one producer who tossed the script at him when he refused to renew the option. When we started working together, we had to gather all the documentation and agreements involved in the previous options, including agreements with the book publishers around the world, to make sure his rights were secure. Without all those documents, examined by our lawyer, we could not have finalized our deal with the financiers.*

Errors and Omissions (E&O) Insurance

An E&O policy is an insurance policy that protects filmmakers, investors, and distributors from any rights' claims, ownership, or defamation complaints from companies or private people.

While the E&O insurance can be obtained at the end of production or right before the sale of the movie, you need to consider the requirements of the insurance company early on, including a cleared chain of title.

Be aware, if you know when you obtain E&O insurance that you have a problem with your chain of title or a claim against the rights to the property, you have to tell the insurance company. They may or may not agree to cover you against that claim, but you are definitely not covered if you don't tell them.

Pitching

Once your IP is secured, it's time to get other people excited about it. As the saying goes, "you don't get a second chance to make a first impression." So if you hope to convince someone to join your project, you'll need to find a way to pitch it, make a case for it, and get people as enthusiastic about it as you are. Some pitches come easily, especially if you have a "high concept" idea or if it is based on a well-known person, book, or story. But even so, you'll need to show your specific point of view for the story and why you believe in the project's potential and relevancy, both artistically and commercially.

It takes time to perfect your pitch. I improve it by pitching it over and over to others and to myself. Each time I pitch it, I learn something about the project itself as much as I learn how my pitch is being perceived. Personally, I love meeting people in person to pitch my ideas; and then I complement it with a deck or a sizzle reel to portray the overall vision. Think about pitching as a trailer for the movie you are going to make. It needs to be captivating.

When creating your pitch, it's important to define who this pitch is for as well as the purpose of it. Is it more of a creative pitch to entice a director or an actor, or is it for a production company or private financier? The spirit of the pitch stays the same. However, you might emphasize different elements. For instance, if it is for producers and financiers, add more details about the financial plan for the movie. On the other hand, if this is directed more to an agent of an actor or the actors themselves, you should give more focus to the character descriptions.

Pitch Meeting

In person pitch meetings are a performance. You want to get people excited about your idea and fill the room with creative energy. I usually would start with some small talk but veer very quickly to start the pitch. I start with the title, the tagline, and the current stage of development of the project. I then briefly describe the plot, and then, most importantly, I talk about what the project is about and why I am personally so passionate about it.

What you hope for from a successful pitch meeting is that they ask to review more materials, to have subsequent meetings, and a general feeling that you were able to boost curiosity about the project.

But you also want to leave the impression that you are a reliable, professional potential partner. Making a movie with someone is a major commitment and a long-term engagement, so what you bring into the room is not only the pitch of the project but also yourself as someone people will want to partner with.

✤ *When we pitched* Wedding Bell Blues *to Todd Fisher, legendary actress Debbie Reynolds' son, he laughed and told us that if the script turned out to be as good as the pitch, he'd allow the whole cast and crew to stay in his hotel in Vegas for free and film in his casino. Todd said he'd even convince his mom to make a cameo if we wanted to write in a role for her.*

This promise was beyond exciting as shooting in a casino is prohibitively expensive and a very complex operation. Being a low-budget film, free rooms, food, and location amounted to at least half of the movie's budget. Having Debbie Reynolds in our cast added legitimacy to the project and helped create a "buzz" among agents and managers, which led to casting the main roles with wonderful actors. We were so lucky. Thank you Todd!

The tagline was something like, "To get their families off their backs, three friends decide to go to Vegas to find husbands and then get divorced ... all in one weekend." We continued by telling the origin of the story, what it meant to me personally, and how the movie is really about those women finding the confidence to be their true selves rather than succumbing to society's expectations. After the successful meeting, we rushed to complete the script, wrote a fun role for Debbie, and the movie took off.

Pitch Deck

Here are some of the elements I use when I create a pitch deck. Whether it is a creative pitch deck or a business plan pitch, many elements remain common.

- The title of the project should give a hint as to the genre of the movie.
- Identify the IP and mention the current stage of development of the project.
- The tagline is an enticing line which should identify who is the main character, their goal, adversity and moral dilemma.
- A short description of the plot, including the moral dilemma or moments of decision of the main character.
- A brief description of what the movie is really about. Identify its "theme," and list a couple of movies that relate to the deeper meaning the movie is exploring.
- Share your director's vision. Talk about your passion and personal connection to the project.
- Potential actors—add pictures of your wish list for leading roles.
- Share bios of the director, producer, writer, and anyone else who's attached.
- Explain the business plan for the project, including any secured elements you might have, such as talent, locations, music rights from famous artists, or any other element that might help the financing of the movie. You should detail whether partial funds have been committed to the project and where you intend to film. Are you anticipating tax incentives, etc. Basically, show that you have a viable financial plan. You might want to add some market analysis, comparisons with other projects, a potential distribution plan, and the terms of the return on investment for private investors.

- Have visual references for the movie's look and style. You can use images from other movies, drawings and illustrations, and artwork. In fact, the design of the deck should reflect the mood and creative orientation of the project's style, genre, and uniqueness.

Sizzle Reel

The sizzle reel is your proof of concept. Think of it as a trailer to the movie you have not yet made, highlighting the story, style, and mood, all within, on average, two minute video. You want to capture your audience and evoke their curiosity. It has to be riveting and cut through for people to see the artistic and commercial value of the project.

Since the reel is for private viewing only, you can utilize music and visuals from other movies (no copyright infringement risk as long as you do not post it, advertise it, or expose the materials in any way to the public). You can pair these with narration, quotes from the script or adapted material, and storyboard illustrations to create a cohesive feel for your movie.

❀ *For Jungle, we hired a company that specializes in creating sizzle reels. It included interviews with Director Greg McLean, who said it would be the greatest survival movie of all time. He was clear with his vision, engaging, and charismatic. We added footage from other survival films, which related to our story, quotations from great reviews of the book, storyboards for the extreme action scenes, exhilarating music, exciting shots from Greg's previous movies, and a few shots of actors we hoped would be attached. We screened the sizzle at the AFM (American Film Market) and Arclight Films was able to presell the movie in some key territories, which helped finance the production.*

Sharing Your Original Ideas

Every movie is hard to make, and you never know when and if you will be able to get it off the ground. But some movies will absolutely never ever happen… those are the movies you stop pitching, the ones you stopped believing in, or the ones you overprotect and don't want to share your original idea.

I share my script and stories ideas even years after they have been buried in my drawer. You never know when the opportunity will arise with the right timing and right place. A great project may be relevant years after you developed it. And I am rarely worried about someone stealing my ideas as I always feel that my take and vision are unique and very specific to the way I think, create, and develop my stories.

You cannot protect or register an idea or a concept. However, copyright law protects your scripts, outlines, treatments, stories, and bibles beginning the moment you complete these works. While you do not need to register your work to be protected by copyright, registering your work with the US Copyright Office and/or the WGA will allow you to prove you are the author of the work as well as when you authored it.

And it is a good idea to follow up any pitch meeting with an email detailing the content of the meeting including the idea discussed. (Note: While mere ideas are never protected by copyright, they can be protected when communicated in a formal pitch.) Even a casual email mentioning the name of the project, the tagline, and how excited you are about the prospect of discussing it further will give you some protection. It is a good idea to cc your lawyer when sending such a confirmation email as well.

Start the Buzzzzzz

Throughout the movie-making process, you want to raise awareness of your project.

So if you secured the rights for a great IP, you might want to hire a publicist who will attempt to get you "an announcement" in one of the leading professional publications, referred to as "the trades."

You might make several announcements for the same movie at different stages, such as when you lock financing and set a date, when you attach actors, and when you secure distribution.

Making an announcement will call attention to your project within the industry and might generate interest from some production companies, the agents who represent potential cast, and perhaps even film distributors. Beyond that, you'll do really well on IMDbPro for a couple of weeks.

To start a buzz around your project, you can begin by using social media in a smart and sophisticated way, revealing just enough but not too much too early.

In any case, it would be wise to secure a domain name and maybe design a logo or image that will establish a recognizable trademark for your project.

Be in the Know

Keeping up with the rapidly changing landscape of filmmaking is crucial. Regularly reading one or two daily film business publications provides updates on film development, financing, acquisitions, genres, budgets, and actor projects. Even a brief ten-minute daily scan helps familiarize you with industry terminology and keeps you well-informed.

Publications:

- *Deadline*
- *Variety*
- *Hollywood Reporter*
- *IndieWire*
- IMDbPro news

Film blogs and podcasts:

- A wonderful podcast by screenwriters Craig Mazin and John August called Scriptnotes.

Books

For inspiration to follow through and complete your projects, and constantly renew your screenwriting and story telling skills:

- *The War of Art* and *Do the Work* - Steven Pressfield
- *Save The Cat* and *Screenplay and the Screenwriter's Workbook* - Syd Field
- *The Hero with a Thousand Faces* - Joseph Campbell

PART TWO
FINANCING

Financing Indie Films

The Platforms

Territories

Film Markets

Markets at Festivals

Package

Financing

Private Investors

Blue Sky and Securities Laws

Return on Investment–ROI

Tax Deductions for Private Investors

Financial Consultant

Domestic Presales

Foreign Presales

Projections Sample

MG – Minimum Guarantee

Soft Money

International Coproductions

Bank Loan

Gap Financing

Deferred Fees

Completion Bond

Collection Company - CAMA

Profit Participation/Back End

The Waterfall

Waterfall Order Example

Entertainment Lawyer

Open a Company

Be a Deal Maker

Set a Date

Financing Indie Films

Making movies involves high-risk financial investments. In order to attract financing to projects, you must demonstrate a viable business opportunity with a strong likelihood of a minimum return on the investment and the potential to generate profit. As more indie movies are made every year, the competition is brutal. But as the number of outlets and platforms for movies grow, I believe there will always be space for new, innovative, talented voices to create movies that will be noticed and make an impact.

The definition of an indie film is a movie that is made outside the studio system. However, within that very wide scope, some movies are made for millions of dollars with huge stars and others are made for under a hundred thousand dollars in a totally experimental way.

The indie movie business has been shifting rapidly, a change that has become even quicker and more pronounced since the rise of streaming channels, large mergers, and evolving technology. These changes mostly affect the way movies are sold and distributed, as well as the way the audience is consuming them. There will, however, always be a need for content. It was challenging to make an indie movie when I started and it is still challenging. However, if you stay current and up to date you will always find ways to navigate and find opportunities in the evolving world of filmmaking.

Many of the legal and financial terms you will find in this chapter are similar to the terms employed in the world of business and commerce.

The Platforms

Your movie can be exhibited, sold, and distributed to generate revenue on any of these different platforms.

- **Theatrical:** Although the theatrical market is challenging for low-budget movies, a demand and window still exist for creative theatrical releases.

- **TVOD (Transactional Video on Demand):** These platforms allow you to purchase or rent movies individually.

- **SVOD/Premium cable:** This model involves a subscription service where viewers can watch movies as part of their subscription package.

- **AVOD (Advertising Video on Demand):** You can watch movies for free but with advertisement breaks. The AVOD market is growing exponentially as watching movies for free becomes more attractive. Some SVOD companies have also introduced AVOD options on their platforms for a reduced monthly subscription.

- **Boats, Hotels, Airplanes:** Movies can be exhibited in these venues as part of their entertainment offerings.

- **DVD and Blu-ray:** Physical media sales still contribute to revenue.

- **Film Festivals:** Some festivals will pay for screenings and can be a source of revenue.

Territories

Movies are typically sold in the following categories around the world:

- **Domestic Market:** Refers to the United States or all of North America if Canada is included in the rights grant.

- **Foreign Market:** Refers to the rest of the world. Some territories band together to buy movies collectively if they speak the same language, such as Germany and Austria, Benelux (Belgium, The Netherlands and Luxembourg), Latin American countries, or Middle Eastern countries.

- **Worldwide Rights:** Refers to a deal where all rights are licensed to one company for both foreign and domestic markets.

Film Markets

There are three major international film markets each year where sales companies present and sell distribution rights, primarily for independent feature films, to global distributors.

- **AFM (American Film Market):** Takes place in the US every November.
- **EFM (European Film Market):** Takes place in Berlin, Germany, every February, concurrently with the Berlin International Film Festival, also known as the Berlinale.
- **Marché du Film:** Takes place in Cannes, France, every May, alongside the Cannes Film Festival.

During film markets, sales companies promote and sell the films they represent to global buyers, who seek distribution rights for theatrical, TV, cable, and streaming platforms. Multiple buyers from each territory enable competitive negotiations. Sales companies charge filmmakers commissions on sales and fees for market expenses. They set up offices or booths in the hotels or convention centers where the market takes place.

There are other markets such as the **Asian Film Market—Filmart**, which takes place in Hong Kong. Other markets such as **MIPCOM** focus on content for TV programs, as well as coproduction and development deals. It also takes place in Cannes, France in October every year.

Markets at Festivals

Some major film festivals also serve as film markets for domestic sales or worldwide sales. If you are accepted to one of these major festivals, you may receive offers (often multiple offers) and sell your film with the help of an agent or a producer's representative.

Those major domestic festivals are:

- **Sundance Film Festival**: Takes place in Park City, Utah, in January.
- **SXSW Film Festival:** Takes place in Austin, Texas in March.
- **Tribeca Film Festival:** Takes place in New York City in June.
- **Telluride Film Festival:** Takes place in Telluride, Colorado, in early September
- **Toronto Film Festival**: Takes places in Toronto in September.

Some foreign festivals are also known for their movie sales potential, mainly the ones that take place during the film markets such as the Berlin FF and Cannes. Other acclaimed festivals such as Venice Film Festival, Locarno FF, BFI London FF, Busan FF, Tokyo FF are known to be platforms for great exposure and sales opportunities.

Package

In order to finance an indie movie, you should try to create an attractive package.

The terms packaging or package means you have already put together, or bundled up some elements for your movie, which could attract distributors or financiers. The package could include a desired IP, a bestseller, a script written by an acclaimed writer, a great director, and hopefully an actor with a meaningful name who has confirmed their attachment to the movie. An attractive package could also include partial financing that was committed or perhaps an amazing location you were able to secure, sometimes hit songs you secured the rights for or anything else that could make the project enticing.

Most talent agencies these days have a packaging department and agents who specialize in helping producers put their packages together such as making introductions to other financiers or helping introduce the project in a favorable way to actors or stars' agents. The producers can then present the project to distributors or other bigger production companies to help finance the movie. You will need to add a packaging fee to your budget.

It is customary to pay the packaging agency two percent from the budget of the movie (barring some agreed exclusions) with an agreed floor and a ceiling (minimum guaranteed and a maximum spend).

Financing

Financing an indie movie can be as simple as finding one equity investor who pays the entire cost of the movie. However, often your film's financing will be comprised of different elements. Here are some of the components that could be part of your financing plan:

- **Private Investors:** angel investors or private equity.
- **Presales:** If you have a strong package, you may be able to sell your movie before it's made and use the funds for making the movie.
- **Soft Money:** A type of funding that does not need to be repaid.
  - Tax Incentives: Some states and countries offer tax credit or tax rebate.
  - Film Funds: Some foreign countries have funds to support filmmakers.
  - Product Integration
  - Crowdfunding: Platforms such as Kickstarter, Indiegogo.
  - Nonprofits: Nonprofit organization contributions or fiscal sponsors.
- **Bank Loans:** This financing needs collateral in the form of tax rebates, or a minimum guarantees (MG) against presales.
- **Gap Financing:** A higher interest loan that could cover the last twenty percent of the budget.
- **Bridge Financing:** Intermediate funds can pay expenses while financing is secured.
- **Deferred Fees**

Private Investors

The ideal way for a true indie low-budget movie to be financed is with a private investor(s) that can cover one hundred percent of the cash amount needed for the budget. Potential investors can be anyone who wants to support the arts or champion the cause or the subject matter of your project as well as anyone who wants the experience of participating in making a movie, hanging out on set, and walking the red carpet.

The most important points to agree upon are:

- The amount of the investment and whether it will cover the full budget.
- The cash flow and withdrawal schedule.
- Creative Control: Private investors will usually ask for final approval on the key cast members, final cut rights, and approval on key creative hires.
- Return on Investment (ROI): Private investors will be in a priority position in the waterfall (the repayment schedule). Interest on the investment is customary for a private equity investor to receive non-compound interest on their investment.
- Profit—After receiving their investment back plus interest, it is customary that investors share profits with the talent group in a ratio of fifty percent to the investors and fifty percent to the talent pool.
- Credit—Usually an investor will receive an executive producer credit, or a producer credit if they are actively producing per the PGA guidelines.
- Sales of the Movie—The private investor will usually retain the final decision in terms of accepting any distribution deal.

Blue Sky and Securities Laws for Private Investors

Blue sky laws were created after the stock market crash during the Great Depression. They are designed to protect investors from buying securities that are worthless—backed by nothing more than the blue sky. Therefore, securities laws require you to be completely candid with your investors about the risk of the investment.

When I approach private investors, I am always transparent about the fact that as a high-risk venture there is a chance they will not recoup their entire investment.

Any time you take money from someone who won't be involved in the business and promise them a return on investment, you are creating a security under federal law and the law of any state in which you received money. Because you now have a security, you must obey both federal and state securities law. The state securities laws are called "blue sky laws."

Luckily, exemptions are available so you don't have to complete reams of paperwork to meet the Blue sky laws or the laws set by the Securities and Exchange Commission (SEC). To do this, you should only take money from what are referred to as "accredited investors," basically people who can afford to lose the investment. Securities and Blue sky laws can get very complicated. Make sure you consult a securities lawyer about your fundraising.

And remember *do not* take money from those who are not in a financial position to lose it. *Do not* raid your grandmother's retirement fund or your friend's college fund.

Return on Investment (ROI) for Private Investors

Usually, the equity investor will receive their investment back pro rata, or pari passu in the case of more than one private investor, as well as interest on the amount or a negotiated premium. Interest rates on investments are usually one or two percent above prime or a flat ten to twenty percent.

- **Pro rata**: in Latin, means in proportion, meaning the ROI will be in proportion to the amount invested compared with the other investors.
- **Pari passu**: also from Latin, means in equal pace, side by side. It means that all the investors are repaid at the same time.

If you get your investors their money back, many of them will be happy to reinvest in your subsequent movies. Investors will appreciate knowing you are taking precautions to secure their investment, such as obtaining a collection company and a completion bond. However, to maximize the chances for a return and profit, the package is the key.

❀ *I've been very lucky through the years to have some affluent equity investors who were very enthusiastic to invest substantial amounts in my films. Those investors came from a variety of backgrounds, but all shared the passion and excitement of participating in the filmmaking journey, a unique experience they would not normally be involved in with their respective business fields. There is definitely something to be said for the "cool factor" of the film business that makes a risky investment less worrisome for some.*

The investors I've worked with have ranged from people who've made huge profits from selling companies they created to real estate moguls and even a movie star's ex-wife, who enjoyed spending some of her settlement funds. I am eternally grateful for the support from all of my investors.

Tax Deductions for Private Investors

Before you meet with any potential private investors, speak with a local tax expert and a CPA to explore potential tax benefits for them. Various states in the US and certain countries around the world have created tax laws to incentivize investments in their film and TV industries.

In the US, under IRS Section 181 and 168k, the Tax Cuts and Jobs Act allows investors to take a one hundred percent tax deduction for a qualified feature film or television series the same year of the investment (rather than over the course of several years). The deduction can be made from their passive income earned that same year; however, if the investor is involved in the production, the deduction can also be made from active income. Investors can invest as individuals or as a company.

To ensure that any possible deductions qualify, it is critical to set up your financing structure before you receive any investments.

Financial Consultant—"Finder" of Private Investors

Another way to find private equity is to engage a financial consultant. This is someone who is well-connected with access to people who are comfortable with high-risk investments. Often times these consultants are referred to as finders and their fee is referred to as a finder's fee.

A financial consultant will make introductions between producers and financiers who are interested in investing in a movie. You will usually enter into an agreement with such a consultant that pays them a defined percentage of the funds they help secure, usually ranging between two and a half and ten percent. Often, a consultant will receive an executive producer credit on the movie.

If the consultant introduces you to an investor, and the deal doesn't go through for that project, the terms will also usually require a producer to pay a consultant fee for any other project you may present to that investor for anywhere from three to five years from the original introduction.

Although there are some well-known finders of funds, before they agree to help you, they will require that your project be in advanced development with meaningful attachments. Here is where a good package comes in again.

Domestic Presales–Negative Pickup

If you have an attractive package—such as a star attached and a great genre script—you may be able to engage a domestic producer representative to help secure a distribution deal before making the movie. With a signed deal and a minimum guaranteed (MG) payment from the domestic company, you can obtain a bank loan for up to eighty percent of that MG amount. This loan can then be used as part of the movie's financial plan. The domestic distributor will pay the MG upon delivery of the completed movie, allowing you to repay the bank loan at that time.

This process is often referred to as a "negative pickup." It involves making a deal for a studio to buy the movie once it's ready, with the price guaranteed. The term originated from the days when movies were shot on film and the final cut was made from the original negative.

A back-stop deal is a type of domestic presale deal that provides the flexibility to cancel the agreement if another distributor, studio, or mini-major offers to release the movie on a larger scale. These deals are usually for less money than desired but include the option to exit the deal after repaying the advance and a cancellation fee or what we call a "kill fee."

❀ *On the movie Jungle, we were able to presell the movie once we had Daniel Radcliffe attached. We used the guaranteed amount (MG) from the sale, to obtain a bank loan, which we used as part of the financing of the movie. Once the movie was completed, we screened it to a few bigger studios to see if one of them would want to pick it up. People loved the movie but the offers we received were not substantial enough to "kill the deal" with our original distributor. Then once we delivered the movie, the collection company received the guaranteed amount and paid the loan amount (with interest) back to the bank. See, not complicated at all.*

Foreign Presales & Projections

Foreign sales companies specialize in selling indie films globally, either before or after production. They sell distribution rights for platforms such as TV, cable, theatrical, and streaming. Essentially, these companies act as international sales agents, charging around a fifteen percent commission on sales, plus market expenses.

A foreign sales company may presell the film to buyers in a few main bigger territories to help finance the movie. However, committing to a project before it's made contains some risk-taking as the outcome depends on execution. To mitigate risk, the sales company assesses the film's "package" to see if it's attractive enough for presales.

The sales agents will work on projections and evaluations, estimating potential sales in each territory, for potential presales of movies depending on their package and attachments and for completed movies based the same parameters but also based on how the movie turned out. The projection sheet will show an "ask" (maximum) and "take" (minimum) price for each territory with the "take" being the more realistic figure for budgeting.

When evaluating sales projections based on attached actors, other factors like genre, the size of the role, and whether the actor plays the hero or villain can result in different projected numbers, even for the same actor.

Prior to attending the markets, the sales company creates one sheet with details about actors, director, producers, artwork, as well as a video previz, similar to a sizzle reel if they intend to presell the movie or a trailer with the real footage from the movie if it was already completed or while it is in postproduction . If the movie is completed, the sales company will set up screenings for the buyers at market's theaters

As a film maker, if you want to attend one of the markets, you should research to see which one of the sales companies specialize in the genre, and budget level of the movie you are pitching. Try to set up appointments prior to the market, send an email with the information about your movie including the sizzle reel, or deck if available. Don't barge into an office and interrupt a meeting. It is more likely that you will be able to set up a time for the last day of the market, when most of the deals have been made and the sales agents are open to hear about new projects.

❀ *Arclight Films, headed by Gary Hamilton, was my partner on Jungle and also the foreign sales company. Once we attached Daniel Radcliffe to the lead role, they presold the movie to territories like Splendid Film in Germany and Umbrella Entertainment in Australia. We used those contracts to secure a bank loan. Once the movie was delivered, a collection company retrieved the owed amounts, paying off the loan.*

On another favorite project of mine, Rock and Roll Nanny, we made a generous offer to a well-known actor. However, his agent requested one million dollars per week for five weeks. The foreign sales company I was working with argued that since the movie was a family film, the actor's value did not warrant paying such a high amount. Had the movie been a thriller, they would have happily been willing to pay even a higher fee. The deal fell through, and the following year, the actor starred in a major family film. Who knew... It's a business full of surprises. I still believe in the script and will one day make it happen.

On the next page, you'll find a sample of an international sales company's estimate for a low-budget film. Territories may vary.

Projections Sample

TERRITORY	HIGH	LOW
ENGLISH SPEAKING		
United States	N/A	N/A
Canada	45,000	20,000
United Kingdom	85,000	50,000
Australia/NewZealand	60,000	30,000
South Africa	30,000	15,000
Sub Total English Speaking	**220,000**	**115,000**
EUROPE		
Benelux	65,000	25,000
France	150,000	50,000
Germany/Austria	175,000	85,000
Switzerland	15,000	5,000
Greece/Cyprus	10,000	3,000
Ireland	5,000	2,000
Italy	85,000	40,000
Portugal	20,000	10,000
Scandinavia	50,000	25,000
Spain	75,000	30,000
Sub Total Europe	**650,000**	**275,000**
EASTERN EUROPE & CIS		
CIS/Baltics	70,000	30,000
Bulgaria	10,000	5,000
Czech/Slovak	25,000	10,000
Ex-Yugo	20,000	5,000
Hungary	25,000	10,000
Poland	75,000	20,000
Romania	25,000	10,000
Sub Total Eastern Europe	**250,000**	**90,000**
LATIN AMERICA		
Pan Latin America (PTV)	75,000	35,000
Argentina/Para/Uruguay	25,000	10,000
Brazil	50,000	25,000
Central America	20,000	5,000
Chile	15,000	5,000
Colombia	15,000	5,000
Mexico	50,000	25,000
Peru/Bolivia/Ecuador	20,000	5,000
Venezuela	5,000	0
Sub Total Latin America	**275,000**	**115,000**
ASIA		
Pan Asian PTV	50,000	15,000
China	75,000	20,000
Hong Kong/Macao	20,000	10,000
India/Pakistan	25,000	10,000
Indonesia	40,000	15,000
Japan	100,000	50,000
Malaysia	25,000	5,000
Philippines	25,000	10,000
Singapore	15,000	5,000
South Korea	75,000	30,000
Taiwan	40,000	15,000
Thailand-Vietnam	30,000	15,000
Sub Total Asia	**520,000**	**200,000**
ASIA MINOR		
Israel	20,000	10,000
Middle East	50,000	20,000
Turkey	40,000	15,000
Sub Total Asia Minor	**110,000**	**45,000**
ANCILLARY		
Airlines	65,000	15,000
Sub Total Ancillary	**65,000**	**15,000**
TOTAL WORLDWIDE	**2,090,000**	**855,000**

MG—Minimum Guarantee

A minimum guarantee (MG) generally refers to a commitment from a distributor or sales agent to pay the producer a certain amount for the exclusive rights to distribute their movie in a specific region for a certain amount of time. If the agreement between the producer and the distributor is made before the movie is filmed, that commitment can help finance the movie entirely or partially. The distributor can either pay the MG in advance or provide a letter of commitment for the producer to be able to obtain a loan from a bank or other lenders against it.

In other words, when domestic rights or international rights to specific countries are sold prior to making the film, i.e., presold, the distributor who licenses those rights will customarily give you a ten percent cash advance and provide a letter guaranteeing the amount they will pay when you deliver the completed movie. This guarantee to pay is referred to as a Minimum Guarantee (MG). The producer or the sales agent will then be able to monetize up to eighty to ninety percent of the MG and receive a bank loan against it.

If the foreign sales company is very confident in the package and the movie's potential, they may choose to offer a minimum guarantee prior to actually selling the rights to any distributors and base the MG on their estimates.

The distributors or sales agents who had committed to the MG, will be obligated to pay it in full regardless of the success of the movie.

Soft Money

Soft money refers to any contribution to the financing of the picture that does not need to be repaid. Many states and countries all over the world offer great tax incentives to attract production to help their economies grow. This contrasts with hard money, which refers to investments that need to be recouped, usually with interest, or a bank, gap, or bridge loans.

Securing soft money is also an incentive to attract investors, as in most cases no repayment is needed in the waterfall, thereby lowering their exposure and giving them a higher chance of recouping their investment.

Soft money usually comes in the form of:

- Tax Incentives
- Film Funds and Grants
- Nonprofit Organizations
- Product Integration

Tax Incentives

Tax incentives are tax credits and rebates that many states in the US and countries around the world offer to production companies in order to attract filming in their location. They usually offer a certain percentage of the actual expenditure on local crew, equipment, catering, hotels etc. You should call the film commission office in whatever location you are considering to get the details as everywhere is different.

As you consider where to film based on the incentives, research whether enough film infrastructure, equipment rental companies, crew, and local cast are available for you to make your movie.

❀ *When we were getting into production on Breakwater, Ed Winters, one of the producers, had flown to Wilmington, North Carolina, to start setting up the production. I will never forget the Zoom call we had with him while he was sitting all alone in a huge, empty office space. The town was busy with productions and it was incredibly challenging to find equipment and crew.*

We didn't know what to do and even considered pushing the shoot. However, not shooting meant taking a risk of never having all the elements align again: the financing, the momentum, and the cast availability. We decided to move ahead but ended up having to bring some of the equipment and crew from Atlanta, LA, and New York. This was costly and complicated; however, the locations were stunning, the local crew was professional and dedicated, and the incentives were worthwhile. So be aware that if a location is attractive to you, it's also attractive for many other productions.

Film Funds and Grants

Film funds and grants are available worldwide. Some are government-funded, some are regional, and some are offered by nonprofit organizations that want to support storytelling on a specific subject and/or social issue. Every fund or grant has its own application criteria. Some help finance the writing and development period while others help finance the making of the film. Although funds and grants are highly competitive, getting one is hugely beneficial to your project. To be selected for grants from the film funds is a stamp of approval, lending the project credibility, which might help attract additional sources of financing. Some of the funds and grants do not require a return from the film proceeds while others do but in a lower position in the waterfall (after the investors, distributors, deferred fees, and filmmakers).

Nonprofit Organizations

Funding obtained through nonprofit organizations that support a cause your film could help raise awareness for, do not require return on their contribution, and such money is not considered an investment. Some filmmakers open nonprofit organizations for projects promoting certain social issues.

- **Fiscal Sponsors:** Existing nonprofit organizations could be used to secure fundings from individuals, foundations, government, or corporate sources that give only to nonprofit organizations with IRS tax-exempt status.

- **Crowdfunding:** Through companies such as GoFundMe, Kickstarter, and Indiegogo, you could raise funds. You'll need to work on a campaign and create a following who will be willing to contribute. You'll need to assess whether the amount of time, energy, and effort will be worth the amount you'll be able to raise, taking into consideration the company's fees, taxes, etc.

Product Integration

Product integration is a great way to add financing to a movie without having to repay those funds. Money from product integration is basically free money. Many companies and agencies have marketing budgets to spend on integrating the products they represent into the entertainment business. These companies analyze a script and identify which products may be appropriately integrated. The expectation is for the filmmakers to write a scene integrating the product in a meaningful and noticeable way, not merely on a sign in the background. Naturally a contemporary movie will have lots of products to integrate while a gladiator movie might not. No one was driving a Tesla in Roman times.

However, this arrangement is only applicable if a movie or TV show has already secured a substantial theatrical release or a TV, cable, or streaming premiere and if big-name actors are attached.

Sometimes you'll be able to find smaller brands that may want to promote their products even if you do not have a distribution deal but your movie shows potential. Perhaps a promoter of a new indie band is willing to pay you to feature their song in your film, a new power drink, a piece of software, or any other product with financial backing that is willing to spend funds in alternative ways.

Eva Green, gazing at Daniel Craig's watch on the train in the James Bond film *Casino Royale*, said, "Rolex?" And his reply, "Omega," could not have been a better advertisement for the brand. And who can forget the iconic scene in ET with the Reese's candies in the forest? The production received one million dollars for it, and weeks after the movie's release, sales of Reese's candy rose by sixty-five percent. Recently, some movies have received tens of millions, creating memorable scenes, and we are all exposed to massive amounts of advertising.

❀ *Even I found myself becoming a fashion victim when I bought myself Manolo Blahnik shoes for a movie premiere after watching Sex in the City.*

Product Placement

Some companies may be willing to supply or loan different products for free to be used and placed in different scenes. They may not pay for it but the production can benefit from using the products such as computers and other electronics, cars, different drinks, clothes, makeup, the list is endless.

❀ *Jeff Franks, a branding expert, got us many product placements for* Wedding Bell Blues, *including a couple of brand-new Toyotas to drive back and forth to Vegas as we were all driving old jalopies back then. The company's executives were upset with the miles we put on the cars, but then, they were ecstatic when Jeff sent them pictures of the cars with Paulina Porizkova posing beside them, and they got their 'miles' worth.*

International Coproductions

An official coproduction treaty involves two or more production companies from different countries that enter into a formal agreement to work together on a project. This agreement must comply with the specific rules and guidelines set out by the countries involved, which often include meeting certain content requirements, cultural and investment criteria and key creatives and crew hires from the different countries. By adhering to these coproduction treaties, the production can benefit from significant access to different funding bodies, tax incentives, and distribution opportunities that might not be available without the collaboration. The exact benefits and requirements vary depending on the specific treaties of the countries and regions involved.

❀ *Acclaimed writer, director, and producer Eran Riklis creates commercial movies with great artistic value. His films' international appeal enabled him to leverage the different coproduction treaties for his last eight movies.* Reading Lolita in Tehran, *based on the NY Times bestseller, was made as an Israeli-Italian coproduction shot in Rome, while post-production was split between both countries. It received funding from the Yehoshua Rabinovich Tel Aviv Foundation for the Arts and the Creative Europe Programme of the European Union. Though complex to put together, this sensitive, important, and relevant film now resonates globally*

Explaining the coproduction process, Riklis recalls: "In 2002, a German producer approached me about future projects, looking for coproductions with Germany and France. What is a co-production, I asked. I had no idea what that was, but she said, 'A good story that can travel.' So I proposed The Syrian Bride, *which is about a Druze bride and a Syrian groom in Israel. Surprisingly, she loved it, as did her producing partners in Germany and France. The $2.5 million budget was equally raised from Israel, France, and Germany. In Israel, funding came from the National Film Fund, a TV station, and a distributor; in France, Canal Plus, ARTE France, and the film fund; in*

Germany, from ARTE Germany, the NRW film fund, and a distributor. We also secured an MG from an international sales company.

"Following coproduction rules, we filmed in Israel, the cinematographer was German, post-production work was done in Germany, and sound mixing in France. The film was a worldwide success, earning numerous awards. Putting together coproduction deals is a process that requires a lot of attention to detail, patience, and knowledge. Still, it's very rewarding, and the cultural meeting between creative people worldwide is truly inspiring."

Bank Loan

A bank loan is a means by which you borrow money from a bank to help cash flow the production. Later, when you receive revenues from exploitation of the film, you have an obligation to repay the bank loan plus negotiated interest and fees.

Producers can obtain a bank loan against the following guarantees and collaterals.

- **Distributor's advances:** Minimum Guarantees (MG) against domestic and foreign presales.
- **Tax Credits, Incentives and Presales:** For example, the film commission in your shooting location will calculate the estimated tax rebate that you will receive when the movie is completed based on the movie's budget and the amount spent in that country or region. The bank will accept the film commission's calculations and guarantee as collateral for a loan. When the movie has been completed and the film commission has been able to audit the cost report and verify the amount that was spent by the production in the region, they will issue payment to the bank or other lender to cover the loan.

Banks do not take any risk on the success of the film. They want their money back, including interest, whether the movie sells and makes profits or not. That's why they will only give a loan against collateral or any other guaranteed payments. To get a bank loan, you will be required to engage a completion bond company to guarantee the delivery of the movie so the MGs will be honored and the bank can be paid.

Gap Financing

Gap financing is another way to borrow funds to complete financing of the movie.

A "gap" is basically the difference between the budget and the amount you have actually raised. Producers often try to obtain a gap loan to make up the difference.

For example, once eighty percent of your financing is secured, a sales agent with a strong relationship with a lending bank may be able to secure a loan to fund the remaining twenty percent of your budget. The collateral for the loan would be the sales agent's estimates/projections for unlicensed (unsold) territories. However, understand that the bank will engage only with well-established sales companies with proven reputations and will still closely analyze the validity of the sales agent's estimates. A gap loan is more expensive with higher interest than a regular bank loan.

As mentioned, a gap loan will usually be the last piece of financing you arrange. It will require a priority position in the waterfall, which means it must be repaid before equity investors, deferred fees, and everyone else. And in order to receive a gap loan, you will need to engage with a completion bond company and a collection company.

A bridge loan is a type of loan from a bank, other entities, or private lenders who will agree to cash flow the production needs ahead of closing the production financing. It is a high-interest loan, but it is often necessary in order to give offers to actors, finance rewrites, or fund preliminary scouts. This loan allows you to start preproduction while you attempt to close all the legal documents necessary for the movie's financing.

Deferred Fees

On a low-budget indie movie, you can often convince talent and crew to defer a portion of their fees so that more funds can be spent on the elements that actually end up on the screen. This happens when people are passionate about a project and believe in its potential either artistically or financially. Sometimes movie rental companies that want to support young filmmakers will defer their rental fees or services as well.

Deferred amounts will be paid back in a preferable position in the waterfall from the revenues derived from the sale of the movie. This may be before or after investors recoup. Again, it is important for everyone to understand that if the film doesn't generate sufficient revenue, the deferred payments may never be made.

❀ *Wedding Bell Blues happened due to the generosity of so many people and companies. We received a full camera package from Panavision, and all grip and electric equipment from Tom Stern, Clint Eastwood's legendary cinematographer. We got to mix the movie at Skywalker Sound located on George Lucas's ranch in Marin County and obtained full postproduction services from one of the biggest post experts in town, Moshe Barkat, all for little to no upfront fees and a reasonable deferment plan.*

All these people are huge supporters of the arts and see helping young filmmakers as a great mission. The cast and crew all worked for minimum SAG fees against deferment as well. Annette, Ram, and I also deferred our fees and took only three thousand dollars each as salary for that entire year. Luckily the unemployment office in North Hollywood was a couple of blocks away from the editing room. Without the enthusiastic support of all of these people, the movie would not have been made.

Completion Bond

A completion bond is a guarantee from an insurance company (a bond company) to the film's lenders and/or investors to complete and deliver the film on time and on budget if the producer is unable to do so. The concept is very similar to completion bonds in the construction industry, which guarantee to a lender that the building will be completed on time and on budget.

You will be unable to obtain a bank loan or other gap financing unless a completion bond is in place. The bond usually costs about two and a half percent of the film's budget, excluding some above-the-line fees such as the IP, writer's fees, all producer's fees and sometimes director's fees, basically all fees that will not have to be repaid if the movie goes over budget.

Before bonding a film, the bond company will carefully review the production plan and require meetings with the director, producer, AD, line producer, and DP to make sure everyone approves the budget and schedule and feels comfortable they can deliver the movie on time and on budget. The bond company will visit the set to see that everything is running smoothly. If and when they feel that filming is not going according to plan (i.e., delays in the schedule or the film is over budget), they will take preventative steps. If those don't help, they might have to replace the director or the line producer or even the DP, depending on where they identify the problem to be.

While the completion bond guarantees that all scenes in the script will be shot the way they are written, it cannot guarantee the quality of the movie or its success.

Collection Company—CAMA

On independently financed pictures, it usually behooves you to hire a special company who, as a trusted neutral third party, receives revenues from all sources that generate income from the distribution, exhibition, and other exploitation of the rights of the movie. These companies are referred to as collection account managers or CAM's. After receiving the monies into a so-called collection account, the CAM disperses such revenues pursuant to the terms of a collection account management agreement (CAMA) that has been negotiated by the producer with lenders, investors, recipients of deferrals and/or profit participants. The CAMA contains the waterfall for the film.

In order to make sure all accounting is clear and accessible, the CAM will open a separate collection account for each specific project.

Of the few companies that provide CAM services these days, Freeway Entertainment is one of the most notable ones. The CAM's fee typically consists of a setup fee, payable from the first revenues received into the collection account in combination with a sliding scale-based commission that starts with one percent of the amounts they collect, depending on the number of revenues, with the percentage decreasing from there. Depending on the size and complexity of the film, the fees may differ from the aforementioned.

I recommend engaging a CAM early in preproduction for a number of reasons.

- The investors and anyone who has any financial interest in the movie will feel protected as the revenues will be split and paid, reported fairly and in a timely manner based on the signed agreements.

- The traditional US guilds—SAG-AFTRA, DGA, and WGA—may require the establishment of a collection account managed by a CAM so they know the accounting will be handled properly and the residuals will be distributed on time and in a proper manner to their members.

Profit Participation/Backend

In independent filmmaking, "profits" refers to the amount that will remain to be shared between the participants after the payment of all financial obligations, including collection account fees, guild residuals, distribution commissions and expenses, bank loans (and/or gap or other loans), equity investment (plus premium), other expenses and any deferrals.

Net profit definitions are not set in stone. They can vary from film to film, and the particulars are critical to the chances of receiving a profit. For example, some studios and other production companies will try to include an overhead charge in the waterfall before getting to net profits. The position in waterfall will define when and if you will receive net profits.

When negotiating your individual profit definition, it is always good to marry" your own definition to that being offered to the investors and/or to the top talent level providing services on the film.

A common agreement for profit split between private equity investors and producers would be 50/50: fifty percent to the financiers (to be shared pro rata, pari passu, or perhaps "last in first out" among them) and fifty percent to the creative participants in the film (director, producer, writer, actors, HODs, finders, EP, and anyone else who contributed).

The Waterfall

The waterfall is the financial structure that sets out how the revenues earned from the sales and exploitation of the movie are dispersed. A waterfall will include everyone who has a financial interest in the film—private investors, sales companies, banks, the collection company, the different guilds, all of those who deferred payments and of course, actors and all the creators of the movie who have any profit participation.

The waterfall is set forth in a legal document to be signed by all of the above people and entities. It is then shared with the collection company that collects and distributes the revenue from the film. That revenue is then distributed to all parties who are part of the waterfall, in the order set forth therein.

Waterfall Order Example

Here is a brief example of the waterfall order, which the CAM will handle. Different financial structures will have different order in the waterfall.

- The CAM for its fees and expenses
- Private or institutional loans and/or the gap loan if any, plus interest (provided that a bank gives the production a loan, the bank will typically recoup the loan plus interest, costs and expenses in first position, prior to payment to CAM, residuals, etc.)
- Residuals to the different guilds. The actual amount of residuals are calculated by a payroll house that will receive monies from the CAM, from a residual reserve created in the waterfall, and whereby the payroll house cuts the checks and distributes payments to the individual guild members
- The foreign sales agents and the domestic distributors commissions
- Foreign and domestic agents and distributors expenses
- The private investors for the total amount of their investment plus interest in a pro rata, pari passu manner between them
- Deferred fees, if any, are paid to talent and or companies who agreed to defer all or part of their fees and get paid from generated revenues.
- Net profits, whatever is left after all of the above has been paid, will be considered as net profits and will be divided between the investors and the talent pool per their contract. Usually, pro rata, pari passu.

It is a great feeling calling someone on the waterfall to tell them their check is in the mail—especially your private investors and those who deferred their fees.

Entertainment Lawyer

The entertainment lawyer you hire performs a crucial role in all stages of your production, and the earlier you involve them, the better prepared you will be.

When you engage a lawyer to represent the production and handle the production deals, contracts, and legal advice, make sure you agree on a flat fee for the production period including postproduction. Also make sure you and the attorney are clear on the scope of the attorney's services. Below are some of the services the lawyer will provide during development and production:

- Open an LLC dedicated to the project
- Finalize chain of title and assigning IP rights to the LLC
- Finalize contracts with the director, writer, producer, and cast
- Review the deals of heads of departments (HODs)
- Arrange for deal memos for crew
- Draft locations releases
- Finalize deals with service companies
- Finalize the documents for the waterfall

The attorney will help negotiate and finalize your funding deals. You will also need the attorney to review all distribution deals. Whether this is included in your flat fee will most likely depend on the level of complication and sophistication of the deals.

Open a Company

Once you have secured your financing, you should open a single purpose company. It is prudent and customary to open a new company for each project that you make. You can usually close your company three years after a film is released.

It is important to have a new company for each project for:

- **Financial reasons:** Having a dedicated company will allow full transparency of all accounting and will secure against accidental cross-accounting, where the funds of one project are inadvertently used on another project.
- **Liability reasons:** If there are any kind of legal or accidental issues on one movie, it will not affect the other movies and companies (i.e., the person who sues you won't be able to go after your other movies).
- **Tax reporting**

Opening a company is easy. You, your partners, and your lawyer will have to determine the owners/shareholders and managers/officers of said company. If you open the company with partners, you will need a partnership agreement, or at the very least some understanding of how you will interact with your partners—who makes the final creative/business decisions, and how profits are split. You will also have to open an associated bank account and choose a signatory.

Be a Deal-Maker

Raising financing for a film is challenging. When you set out to make a movie, you will have big dreams and aspirations regarding how you want the movie to be shot and budgeted. However, remember the saying, "Be a deal-maker, not a deal-breaker." It is always better to make a movie than to talk about it. My philosophy is when an opportunity arises, take it. I'd rather make a lower-budget movie and get into production than wait years for the ideal financing of my dream budget. Be flexible and creative... Sometimes a limitation can be an opportunity.

Set a Date

Congratulations. You financed your film. It's a huge deal. Now you're ready to set a filming date and begin preproduction.

Part Three: Preproduction

- About Prep "Do the Work"
- Work for Hire
- Producer & Director Agreements
- Above the Line/Below the Line
- The Producer
- Who are All Those Producers
- The Director
- Choosing Where to Film
- Location Manager
- Budget Considerations
- Script Breakdowns & Schedule
- Day Out of Days
- Casting & Casting Director
- Offers to Cast
- Agents & Managers
- Pay or Play Offer
- Auditions
- Production Accountant
- Payroll Company
- Unions
- Insurance
- Workman's Compensation Insurance
- Script Clearance
- Rehearsals
- Director & Director of Photography
- Production Design
- Costume Design
- Hair and Makeup Department
- Transportation
- Catering & Craft Services
- Music Clearance
- Editing Room Set Up
- Scouting with the Crew
- Camera Test Day
- The Production Office
- DOD and Schedule Sample
- Production Meeting

About Prep "Do the Work"

"It's not your job to create your vision; it's your job to have a vision, and then it's your job to hire talented individuals and talented artists who understand your vision."
—Quentin Tarantino

During prep, the producing team and the creative team, led by the director and the heads of departments, engage in many parallel and intertwining activities. In this phase, you will imagine and reimagine the movie. You make many crucial creative and practical decisions utilizing the budget you were able to secure. It will never feel like enough, but you will compensate with creativity, vision, imagination, improvisation, and determination.

Remember the days when you were a kid and everything felt possible? This is how you should approach indie filmmaking. You make it work as you go along. It is stressful, and you work long hours, completely immersed in making the movie. As you hire all the heads of departments and the crew, you will finally collaborate with talented, experienced professionals who are all there to help you bring your vision to life. Some may have more experience than you, so enjoy that privilege as you ask questions, explore options, and try things. This is the time.

I ask questions all the time. I learn and am thrilled when new options are presented that I might not have thought about, and I debate. Some may conceive taking the time to think and contemplate as a weakness, but I disagree. I feel it demonstrates self-confidence, not being closed-minded, and embracing input. And then, when I'm ready, I'll make the decision I feel is right for the movie I am envisioning.

In this chapter I'll try to cover the basic process for the director and producer as they collaborate with the whole production team to prep the movie.

Producer and Director's Agreements

Among the first agreements to be negotiated are the producer and directors. Here are some of the main points to be considered:

- Fee: The fees paid to the producer and a director are commonly based on a percentage of the budget of the film with a floor and ceiling. Often, the fee will be around five percent of the budget each. It is important to pay attention to whether the fee is calculated based on the full budget or only the below-the-line budget of the movie, which can be significantly less.

- Define who has final cut and creative control, including the choices of the main cast members and head of departments.

- Define at what point the producer and director become exclusive to the production and when or if they become pay or play (defined below but basically meaning they must be paid even if the movie is not made).

- Number of days for filming and number of weeks for editing.

- Perks: Terms of travel, accommodations, per diem and personal assistant.

- Backend and profit participation definition and percentage.

- The credit for the producer and director, and where they will appear on screen.

- Who will be awarded company credit.

- Bonus payment if there is a sale to streamers above a certain amount.

- Remakes and sequel rights.

- Inclusion in publicity, press, and advertisement.

- Invite to premiere with travel and accommodations.

Topsheet Budget Sample

Acct #	Description			Amount
100 0	Story & Development	1	$	140,100
120 0	Producers Unit	1	$	191,100
130 0	Directoin	1	$	205,000
140 0	Cast	2	$	405,334
160 0	ATL- Travel	4	$	109,025
180 0	Lead Cast Perks	5	$	-
	Total Fringes		$	172,467
	TOTAL ABOVE-THE-LINE		$	**1,223,026**
200 0	Production Staff	6	$	374,205
210 0	Extras & Crowds	8	$	89,340
220 0	Set Design	9	$	106,090
240 0	Construction	11	$	63,966
250 0	Set Operations	11	$	233,983
260 0	Special Effects	14	$	61,644
270 0	Set Dressing	15	$	130,232
280 0	Property	21	$	41,138
290 0	Wardrobe	29	$	102,755
310 0	Makeup & Accessories	31	$	56,546
320 0	Electrical	32	$	113,124
330 0	Camera	34	$	202,397
340 0	Sound & Video	36	$	43,702
350 0	Transportation	38	$	302,359
360 0	Location & Catering	41	$	431,690
370 0	Picture Cars	43	$	22,150
400 0	Animals & Wranglers	44	$	3,300
420 0	BTL Travel	44	$	85,080
	Total Fringes		$	650,694
	TOTAL PRODUCTION		$	**3,114,395**
450 0	Film Editing	46	$	83,783
460 0	Postproduction	46	$	66,500
470 0	Music	47	$	120,000
490 0	Titles	48	$	1,500
500 0	VFX - Misc	48	$	50,000
520 0	Delvery Requirements	48	$	25,000
	Total Fringes		$	37,249
	TOTAL POST PRODUCTION		$	**384,032**
650 0	Misc Charges: Legal, Financing, Visas	50	$	51,000
660 0	Insurance	50	$	45,975
670 0	Publicity	51	$	38,000
	Total Fringes		$	13,600
	TOTAL OTHER		$	**148,575**
	Completion Bond : 2.5%		$	121,751
700 0	Contingency 10%		$	487,003
	Total Above-The-Line		$	1,223,026
	Total Below-The-Line		$	3,647,002
	Total Above and Below-The-Line		$	4,870,028
	Grand Total		$	**5,478,782**

Above the Line/Below the Line

The crew on a movie is divided by title into "above the line" and "below the line." Above the line is a term that includes the top creative positions (i.e., producers, director, writers, and cast). Below the line refers to the rest of the creative heads of departments and the rest of the crew who work on the movie.

These monikers were originally derived from the design of the top sheet, the first page of the budget, that details the overview and total budget of the movie.

- **Above-the-line** section of the budget includes the director, writer, producers, cast, casting director, stunts, and all living and travel expenses for those personnel.
- **Below-the-line** section of the budget includes all other crew, equipment, location, and post expenses. The below-the-line section is divided into the production filming period and postproduction.
- **Other** section includes overhead such as insurance, legal fees, visas, financing charges, bank charges, interest fees, office rentals, marketing fees.

The last section of the budget may include costs calculated as a percentage such as the contingency, customarily set at ten percent and the completion bond at around two and a half percent.

Ultimately, all contracts signed with any person on the movie will have to be characterized as "**work for hire**" as all rights to anything that is created for the movie will need to be owned by the production company in perpetuity to avoid any copyright issues. This will include, as mentioned, all writing agreements, rewrites, actors' services, director and producer agreements, stunts, heads of departments including production designer's work, composer, and still photographer.

The Producer

Throughout prep, the producer will finalize the financing contracts, negotiate with agents, and lock cast deals while supporting the efforts of all the departments. Two of the most important decisions are when to lock the budget and to determine the number of days of filming. Only then can all elements of the production be negotiated and secured. The producer will work very closely with the director to try and support their vision, offer advice, act as a sounding board for ideas, go on scouts, and sit in on auditions.

"The Dream Facilitator"

On every movie, we plan and dream of many artistic, exciting and innovative ways to tell the story. The director, the DP, and other heads of departments may have specific requests for things such as cranes, Steadicam, motion control cameras, anamorphic lenses, insert cars, drones, extravagant stunts, extensive visual effects, extra days of filming, longer hours, and more. These well-thought-out requests could enhance the look of the movie; however, they may substantially impact the budget.

For the young producer who gets annoyed with these requests, don't. It is the job of the director to ask, push the envelope, and find innovative ways to tell the story. And it is the job of the producer to try and find a way to incorporate these requests within the budget or suggest creative alternatives to achieve the vision. However, sometimes difficult decisions will need to be made, and compromises will happen. No matter what the budget of the movie is, you'll need to make tough choices.

❀ *On Look Away, someone heard me negotiating over the phone for anamorphic lenses. After a long, tiring conversation, I said something like, "You have to get me this. I want to facilitate the director's dream." The next day, there was a huge sign on my office door —"Producer Dana Lustig, Dream Facilitator."*

Who Are All Those Producers?

Here is an overview of what the customary definitions of producing credits are.

Producer: The person(s) who will follow the project through from the development of the script through financing, prep, filming, postproduction, and the sale and release of the movie. They are the backbone of the movie and therefore are recognized by the academy to be the only ones eligible for Oscar nomination for Best Picture. The Producer's Guild of America also reserves the trademark, PGA only for the main producers who have been involved in a meaningful way.

Coproducer: A person who is involved in getting the project together. Usually not the initiator of the project but a contributor in some way.

Executive Producer: A person who has helped to put the movie together in one of many ways including arranging for all or partial financing or casting the stars, which as a result, helped finance the movie. It can also be a person chosen on behalf of a big company that produced the movie.

Associate Producer: A person who has contributed to the producing process in some way at any stage of the project that should be recognized. This is often a "thank you" credit.

Line Producer: A person who handles the production budget, the cost report, and deals with all heads of departments. They will hire the crew and handle the physical production tasks to allow the producer the space to deal with the more creative issues.

The Director

For me, being the director of a movie is the best job in the world—one of the most privileged yet one of the most ambitious and demanding. As the creative force of the movie, the director should bring a contagious enthusiasm for the cast, crew, and the entire team to join the journey and participate in the vision.

Every director has their own process; nobody directs the same way. In my case, I'm very thorough. I do a detailed shot list. I meet with my actors and rehearse. But I also like to come to set and throw it all out the window for a moment and see what happens. I ask a lot of questions, and I welcome input from experts. But in the end, it all has to fit into the vision I have set out to create.

During prep and throughout the project, the director will make hundreds if not thousands of decisions and choices. They will form every determination as to the movie's style and look. To convey their vision, a director usually creates a mood board that will serve as a bible for all the department heads and might include pictures, drawings, magazine spreads, music lists, movie clips, pictures of potential cast, etc. This vision helps everyone work toward making the same movie. The director will also work with the writer to refine the script to accommodate production needs or tailor something to a specific actor.

Ultimately the director's job is to take the written script and turn it into a cinematic experience in their own specific style and vision.

Choosing Where to Film

Choosing the country or state where you will film is crucial to start putting your production together and must be considered early on. It will affect your budget, schedule, casting, and crew hiring.

First to consider would be the script and creative needs. Is it an urban movie or a nature adventure? Do you need hot tropical jungles or snowy mountains?

The film commissions of every state and country you might consider will have information regarding tax incentives and grants offered. They can advise whether enough crews and equipment rental companies are available and can make introductions to local production service companies. Some film commissions may offer a free scouting trip to introduce all options to you.

❀ *When I started working on Jungle, Yossi, who was living in Mullumbimby, Australia, told me that the jungles there resemble the ones in Bolivia. I met with the Australian Film Commission in LA and realized that their tax incentives were attractive, and if you had enough Australian elements, the grants were very lucrative. So I flew there and connected with Justin Monjo, one of Australia's top writers, and later collaborated with a local production company.*

Because of this, we qualified to be considered a local production and maximized the incentives. Plus, the Australian crews are top-notch professionals. However, we still needed some locations that Australia did not have. We explored many South and Central American countries and settled on Colombia, whose film commission invited us for a free scouting trip. They also had great film infrastructures and crews, on top of great incentives and a good dollar exchange. So Jungle was shot in both countries.

Location Manager

Once you have chosen where to shoot, the Location Manager will be one of the first crew members you hire during prep as they will scout for your ideal locations per the deck and the director's vision. They will present many options, and after numerous scouting trips the director along with the DP, production designer and producer will choose the locations.

The location manager with the production manager and/or line producer will negotiate the fees and terms for use of the locations. Locations may also need to be rented for prep, wrap, and cleaning days to save time on filming days.

Ideally, some of the locations can double as more than one scene/location in your script. This can save you the cost of both additional locations and, just as important, time to move from one location to another.

The location department is also responsible for setting up base camp and parking in collaboration with the transportation department.

FILMING PERMITS

The location manager will arrange for permits from the permit office in whatever city or town you are filming and will find out any requirements that may be needed such as fire marshals, police presence, water truck, or any other type of safety accommodations. They will also conduct a notification process to all neighbors to make sure there is no resistance from them to you filming in their neighborhood.

Other considerations in choosing a location that a good location manager should be able to spot are potential sound problems in the area, which might disrupt the production sound, such as an airport, highway, school, or train station.

❀ On the film Look Away, which we shot in Winnipeg, Canada, we found the perfect location in a warehouse where we built a couple of important sets. But what no one had taken into account—and we only found out the day of filming—was that the neighboring warehouse was actually a mosque where they would pray five times a day for fifteen minutes each time using a loudspeaker. We were all freaking out. It was almost a disaster, but luckily the imam and the worshipers were extremely nice and accommodating. They agreed to be flexible with their prayer times and took it with a great sense of humor. They wanted to support our filming.

On Breakwater, director James Rowe, who is from North Carolina where we were shooting, was inspired to write the script after a visit to the Outer Banks. James took the initiative and was able to obtain the gorgeous, unique lighthouse at Currituck Beach in Corolla for free for our shoot. As we shot the majority of the movie in Wilmington, which is almost six hours away, that free location ended up being a very expensive one as we had to hire the crew for two travel days plus pay for hotels, per-diem and gas for everyone. In the end it was worth it as that beautiful lighthouse became a character in the movie, but just be aware when you scout that free isn't always free.

Budget Considerations

During the financing period, you will have an estimated budget that you will work from. Once in preproduction, however, you will be working with the actual funds raised and the line producer (LP) will create a cohesive final production budget.

Some of the items that will be taken into consideration when making the budget are:

- The locked amount that is available for production
- Above-the-line cost agreements
- Total days of filming
- Location: if remote, the budget will require travel, accommodations, per diem, and ground transportation
- Number of locations and moves: it is always best to try and combine as many sets as possible in one location to save time on moves
- What camera, how many cameras, which lenses and ratio you choose to use on the film
- Visual effects
- Special equipment, special effects, stunt work, etc.

And any specific needs demanded by the script with regard to genre and scope.

Script Breakdown and Schedule

The first assistant director (AD) will break down the script and mark all the elements that need to be scheduled into a scheduling program. This includes actors, extras, props, special effects, stunts, armor, animals, picture cars, cranes, drones, and more. Each head of department will then create their own more detailed breakdown, which will inform the AD and help them refine the master breakdown.

Based on the breakdown pages, the AD will then create the shooting schedule for all departments. While they will try to schedule filming in script order as much as possible, items like actors' schedules, location availability, weather restrictions, and makeup considerations will take precedent in creating the final schedule.

The director and producer in collaboration with the HOD's will examine the schedule and give their input as to how long they will need to film each scene and any special requirements they may have. The AD will then adjust and create the final schedule. Schedules often change due to unforeseeable circumstances, so flexibility is the key.

And remember, not all scenes are created equal. A three-page scene with two actors talking may take half a day or a day of filming while a three-line scene with a huge fight may take three days. So, not only the number of pages but the content of each scene dictates the schedule.

Day out of Days

The DOD (day out of days) is a chart derived from the schedule that shows in a visual, calendar-like way all the elements that will be needed on any given shoot day—like cast, locations, and special equipment. It is automatically created by the scheduling program based on the script and the AD's breakdown. This will become the bible of production.

As both a director and producer, I always do my own script breakdown, where I go over the script and mark everything needed for a scene in colored highlighters. This helps me familiarize myself with all the details and allows me to plan the production better.

❀ *On Jungle, Daniel Radcliffe played Yossi Ghinsberg, who was lost in the jungle and had to survive for twenty-one days. During his ordeal, Yossi had lost over twenty pounds, so Daniel, prior to filming put himself on a drastic diet, which he continued during the first half of filming in Colombia, eating only one egg and a protein bar a day. Needless to say, he never joined us at the lunch table, and everyone was sensitive not to eat next to him on set.*

Daniel slowly throughout filming had lost weight, so the AD scheduled filming as much as possible in chronological order so that during the final scene of the movie, when Daniel is rescued, he would be looking frail and thin, on the verge of dying. Then we scheduled two weeks off to allow Daniel to gain back some weight. Once we moved production to Australia, we shot earlier parts in the movie going back to the first scenes at the end of the shoot, when he was back to his normal weight. All of this was reflected in the DOD schedule for planning.

Casting and the Casting Director

When casting a movie, you must consider both creative wishes and financial restrictions. Here is where a skilled casting director comes in. They will be a great curator, possessing impeccable taste, a deep understanding of the script, and the ability to identify ideal actors for each role. The casting director also needs to be able to spot new talent and think innovatively for specific roles. A good casting director is familiar with the agencies and talent management companies and stays up to date with actors' work.

The casting director typically creates a long list for each main role: the unrealistic wish list, the more realistic hard-to-get list, and the most realistic list. Once the director, producer, and financiers agree on the list, often with input from distribution companies, the casting director checks the availability of actors for the planned filming time by contacting their agents or managers. They gauge the actor's interest and preferences and decide whether to proceed with an official offer.

A-list and well-known actors usually won't audition for roles in small indie movies. You make an offer and hope they will accept it. They may, however, agree to a creative meeting with the director after receiving a serious offer and reading the script. Those meetings are crucial as the director and actor will talk about the role and get a feel for whether they can inspire one another and collaborate in a visionary manner. As a director, you must come prepared to that meeting as you are likely being auditioned as well.

❀ *When casting* Kill Me Later, *I met with quite a few well-known actors who were all interested in the role of the charming bank robber. We had lovely lunches and deep conversations about the script and the character. I knew I should make an official offer to one of them, but something stopped me. I was waiting for that moment where I would simply know.*

One day, the casting directors, Mary and Karen Margiata, who knew me well and completely got what I was looking for, sent me a couple of scenes of a young British actor, Max Beesly and as soon as I watched them, I knew... it was him! I asked to meet with him, but he was in London wrapping a film where he had played the role of Tom Jones.

So, we set up a long phone meeting where we talked about the role, the different accents for the character, and his background. Max shared that he is also a drummer. That call sealed the deal, and I even went back to the script and added a couple of scenes where Max would drum on the dock near his hideaway boat. Ram and I had to convince the investors, Carol Nemoy and Federico Pignatelli to agree to a lesser-known actor. Luckily, they also saw the star quality in Max and agreed.

When I start working on a movie, I always have an idea for actors for each role. I try to think beyond the predictable type casting and think about the anti-type, an actor who perhaps always plays a villain who might shine in a leading role. I like to think about how each actor can bring something interesting, different, and unexpected to the character. In order for notable name actors to want to engage in an indie movie, the role has to be very intriguing to them.

I remember when, for a certain movie, I called Beth Holden Garland, who was the manager of the late Ray Liotta to check his availability and potential interest. Beth, one of the nicest managers in the business, asked me if this would be a life-changing role for Ray? Would it change his career? Was it a role he had never done before? She told me she would be happy to present him the offer if I thought so. The role was good and even intriguing. We were prepared to pay a decent amount, but it was not a career-changing role, and we ended up with another amazing actor. So, as you start thinking about who to give offers to, try to see if the role will be attractive for the actor.

Offers to Cast

Casting your movie may take months. Only one offer can be made at a time for specific role. You therefore must put a time limit on the offer for the actor to accept or reject it. If you give an official offer to an agent, by law they are obligated to present it to their client, even if they do not recommend that the actor accept the role. The offer will include start date, location, compensation, duration of service, the placement or position of the credit on screen and in advertising, dressing-room-setup, travel and accommodation details (if necessary), and profit participation.

The casting director will send the written offer along with the script and often a letter to the actor written by the director, talking about the role and why they are so excited about the prospect of working with that actor. You can also submit the director's previous work, a sizzle reel, or a deck to give the actor a sense of the creative direction of the movie.

When casting a bigger name actor, there will likely be other terms, including approval of the opposite leading role, exclusive hair and makeup artists, upgraded travel arrangements and sometimes for their family (e.g., private planes and first-class accommodations). Oftentimes they will request extra security.

I have also encountered requests for private chefs, physical trainers, and acting or speech and accent coaches. Although some of these demands may be a heavy load on a low-budget production, you want to accommodate them in order to make your lead actors feel comfortable. Being an actor is to be put in a very vulnerable position, so I understand the demands, and I am happy to find a way to make it happen.

Other terms will be negotiated when the actor accepts the offer and a long form (the full contract) is signed, including availability for reshoots, ADR work, publicity appearances and bonus payments

Agents and Managers

Established actors, writers, directors, and sometimes producers are represented by "talent agents" and sometimes also by "talent managers." Producers and casting directors approach talents through their representatives and check their availability and interest. When the project is financed and you are ready to give a serious offer that you can stand behind, the offer is sent to the actor's agents either by the casting director or your entertainment lawyer.

Each country has local talent agencies, and you can check where each actor is represented by checking their IMDbPro page. As mentioned, the agent is obligated to at least discuss any official offer that the actor might receive even if their recommendation would be to pass. An agency charges their clients ten percent of their fee.

Some actors will also engage management companies in addition to agents, as they usually represent fewer actors at any given moment and can give more personal attention. The manager might help an actor to strategize their goal in the long run, and they read the scripts carefully to help the actor choose the right project. Management companies usually charge the actors around fifteen percent of their fees. Managers are allowed legally to join a project as producers where agents are not permitted to do so.

The agents and managers are actively pitching their clients to producers and directors as they become aware of projects that are in the process of casting. They are an essential part of the movie business. Agencies and management companies may also serve as "producer representatives," through their packaging departments.

Pay or Play Offer

When extending offers to leading roles or stars, it's common to structure them as pay or play offers. This commitment means that the producer is obligated to pay the actor once they commit to the movie, regardless of whether the production proceeds or not. It also means that if you decide to replace the actor after they are made pay or play, you have to pay them their full fee unless they are in breach of contract or there is a force majeure. Offering pay or play adds legitimacy to the project in the eyes of the actor's representatives, signaling a higher level of seriousness. However, only make a pay or play offer when you have the financing available. If you don't, you will likely be sued, and, at the very least, you will lose creditability in the industry.

Once the actor commits to the project, they won't take on any other commitments for the specified time period when filming is scheduled. If the offer isn't backed up, and the movie doesn't materialize, it can result in significant losses for the actor. Upon signing a deal memo, you may be required to deposit a certain percentage of the fee into an escrow account with the actor's agents. The escrow account, controlled mutually by the actor's reps and the production lawyer, ensures the actor's salary will be paid even if the movie doesn't happen and also protects the production company in case the actor for some reason is not able to perform.

"Cast breakage" is a term we use when and if a name actor expresses interest in taking the role in the movie but demands a high fee that exceeds what has been budgeted. In that case, the investors and distributors may consider investing additional funds to accommodate the actor's involvement if they believe the participation of that actor will enhance the financial value of the project.

Auditions

Auditioning is an exciting stage of casting your movie. Except for the A-list actors who won't audition, most everyone else will prepare and rehearse a couple of scenes that you have selected. When actors come to read, it might be the first time you hear some of those scenes performed out loud, and you'll be able to see different interpretations and performances. Sometimes you can do chemistry auditions with two or more actors together to see if the actors are a good match. For smaller roles, recorded or Zoom auditions often work. For the leading roles, you really need to be in the room with the actor to make a final decision. Plan on flying to wherever the actor is, or fly them in to audition.

❀ One of the most mind-blowing auditions I ever witnessed was when Jodie Whittaker (Dr. Who) came in to read for A Thousand Kisses Deep. *The movie follows a woman who travels back in time to undo some of her decisions that were affecting her life. As she travels to the past, she interacts with her younger self. My choice was to have the same actress play both roles, so for the auditions we would have an actress read the other role opposite the actress who was auditioning. Jodie, however, insisted on reading both parts herself. She transitioned between the two versions of the character flawlessly. Every time she changed character, her whole demeanor, voice, and body language changed. She just looked in the other direction, and you knew which role she was doing. It was as if two actresses were performing at the same time.*

During the auditioning process for Dancing at the Blue Iguana—*directed by Oscar-nominated Michael Radford, about a group of women working in a strip club and their complicated lives—Sharon Howard Field, the casting director who has impeccable taste and a sense to recognize great talent, managed to bring famous and well-established actors, all of whom put their egos aside and arrived in full hair and makeup for a three-day auditioning process. I was so touched to see the love and dedication of those true artists putting themselves on the line.*

Production Accountant

The production accountant plays a crucial role in making the movie. On a low-budget movie, they usually work by themselves, but on bigger movies, they will have support (e.g., an assistant accountant).

The production accountant will work with the producer and line producer to finalize the budget and calculate all line items correctly.

- They will be the signee on the bank account and will handle payments, deposits, and opening accounts with the different vendors.

- They will work with all heads of departments and handle all purchase orders, petty cash, weekly payments, and timecards.

- The production accountant will also create a weekly cost report so the producer and investors as well as the completion bond company (if there is one) will always know what was actually spent to date as compared to expected spending set forth in the budget.

- The production accountant, along with the producer, will create a drawdown schedule, which is a predicted schedule as to when funds will be needed as cash flow during prep, production, and postproduction. The funds will need to be deposited in the bank account per that schedule.

Payroll Company

The payroll company handles payment to the entire cast and crew, and they also pay the fringes to the unions and calculate taxes, social security, and pension. Most importantly, they will cover everyone who is paid through their service with workers' compensation insurance.

The accountant will handle the communication with the payroll company. He or she receives the approved time cards for the cast and crew and calculates the amount that will need to be paid to the payroll company to cover those payments. The payroll company will also handle the residual payments to the unions.

Anyone who gets paid through the payroll company will be covered by its workers' compensation policy. However, there are other people visiting the set or working as independent contractors who are not paid through the payroll company, and therefore you should buy an extra workers' compensation policy.

Unions

There are different professional unions for the film industry. Depending on your budget and who your writer and director are, you will determine to which unions you will become a signatory. The relevant US unions are the WGA (Writers Guild of America), DGA (Directors Guild of America), SAG-AFTRA (Screen Actors Guild-American Federation of Television and Radio Artists), Teamsters, and IATSE (represents most professional crew members).

By working with union members, you are guaranteed to work with more professional and experienced people. The unions protect their members rights, ensuring fair hours and safe and healthy working conditions. They also support their members with health insurance and pension savings, which the production will have to contribute to, adding extra payroll costs for the production. The unions have a few rate tiers to accommodate the needs of different budget levels, but this doesn't always offset the additional expense.

Whether they've signed up with any unions or not, production companies need to follow all federal and state labor laws, and if they sign with any of the unions, they need to follow the union's guidelines as well in regard to hours on set, turnaround or rest time, overtime fees and more. You can hire companies, like CMS, to handle your union negotiations and dealings, such as the union signatory process, amounts of deposits, and residuals. This can be very helpful but they charge a fee which would be added to your budget.

- **Residuals:** If your production company signs the collective bargaining agreement with one or more of the guilds, you will be required to pay a percentage of film revenues every time the film is exhibited in any media other than the media for which it was originally made.

Insurance

You will need to obtain different kinds of policies at different stages of production. Don't start prep or shoot without insurance, as accidents happen! Always review the specific needs for your film with an experienced production insurance broker before filming.

The production insurance package will usually (at a minimum) include:

- **Liability:** General liability insurance protects against third-party property damage and injuries.
- **Equipment:** All the rented equipment will have insurance; rental houses will require the certificate of insurance.
- **Vehicles:** Both picture cars and transportation vehicles will be covered.
- **Locations coverage.**
- **Stunts:** Any stunts or dangerous activity need to be disclosed and explained in detail ahead of time. The insurance company will then decide if an extra fee is needed. This could be related to filming with drones, helicopters, car stunts, filming on boats or underwater, fights, falls and anything else which might endanger the cast and crew.
- **Essential Elements Insurance:** This policy covers the production in case something happens to anyone who is "essential" to the completion of the production. "Essential" personnel mainly include the lead actors, the director, and sometimes the DP. Anyone listed on that policy will need to undergo a medical exam in order to be approved and covered. The insurance will cover the production in case of sickness, accidents, and death of anyone listed.

Workers' Compensation Insurance

Workers' compensation insurance provides benefits to employees who get injured or sick from a work-related cause. It also includes disability benefits, missed wage replacement, and death benefits. Workers' compensation also reduces your liability for work-related injuries and illnesses.

Make sure anyone who gets paid through the payroll company will be covered by their workers' compensation policy. Some insurance companies allow independent contractors who are not paid through the payroll company to be covered by a separate policy, so check with your insurance broker.

Do not allow anyone on your crew to work, rehearse, or do anything on your behalf without being covered by workers' compensation!

❀ *On a movie I produced, I was debating between two different WC quotes, and I did not buy the extra insurance prior to the beginning of production. That first morning of filming, the stunt coordinator took one of the picture cars for "a ride" and bumped into an old man driving twenty miles an hour. Luckily neither of them got physically hurt. The picture car was insured under the general liability, but I was scared that the old man would come back to sue us. I didn't sleep all night.*

In my mind I saw how I was losing my house and all my savings. The next day I found out that the old man arrived at night to talk with the security guard on site. He was more frightened than me. Apparently, he was driving drunk out of his mind and thought I would sue him. He went away but not before the guard treated him with goodies from craft services. I purchased the WC insurance that minute and since then, I won't let anyone, I mean anyone, work without being covered.

Script Clearance

Script clearance is a report done by a copyright lawyer who will thoroughly review the script to point out any potential copyright or trademark infringements as well as identifying the risk of defamation. The report will suggest what might need to be changed in the script along with any suggestions to acquire clearances. Some of the elements they may look for are:

- Names of characters, including phone numbers and addresses
- Company names
- License plates
- Street names, street signs, etc.
- Tattoos on actors need clearance from the tattoo artist (or need to be covered)
- Music rights
- Quotes from books, songs, or other movies

The title of the movie will also be researched for clearance for an additional fee.

One of the many requirements to obtain E&O insurance is to show a script clearance report. Without the clearance report, the insurance company will not bind your movie with the necessaray insurance.

Rehearsals

Every actor has their own way of "getting into character" and owning it. During rehearsals, the director and actors have the chance to understand each other's specific processes, techniques, methods, and approaches to building their character. This can be of great assistance later on set when the time is rushed, and the pressure is on. Also, as filming is usually scheduled out of sequence, rehearsals are the only time when you can attempt to work with the actors in script order to follow and build the character's precise arc.

Rehearsals should be the time when actors can feel comfortable to experiment, be brave, and try different takes and approaches to a specific moment without worrying about failing. That is when the unexpected can happen and later be recalled on set.

Time is also set out for actors who need to learn, study, or practice new skills such as learning a musical instrument, a specific accent or language, or how to ice skate, dance, or perform fight scenes.

❀ For Dancing in the Blue Iguana, we rented a small theater for three months. The dedicated actresses Sandra Oh, Daryl Hannah, Jennifer Tilly, Charlotte Ayanna, and Sheila Kelley—who came up with the original idea and now runs the mega successful S Studios, teaching pole dancing as an empowering method for women—would have long rehearsing sessions. They also visited real strip clubs and hung out with the dancers, visited them at home, and tried to live their lives as much as possible. They would then bring their experiences to the rehearsals with Michael Radford and writer David Linter so they could build their characters together.

During rehearsal for Kill Me Later, there was a scene where Max Beesley had to make Selma smile to get her to snap out of her morbid thoughts while watching a funeral procession. A joke written in the script wasn't working. I had this feeling that I might destroy the scene if I pushed too hard, so we moved on to another scene. I then talked to Max privately and asked him how he would charm a woman in a bar... did he have a "go to" line? What's his schtick? He told me, and we chose not to rehearse but to keep it for the set.

When the day came to shoot the scene, Max put the lit side of a cigarette in his mouth and blew. When a lot of smoke came out, he asked the puzzled Selma what she thought it was. She looked amused but perplexed, and he cheekily replied that it was a "choo-choo train." She smiled and we got that moment of enchantment, a genuine true moment on camera in which we could feel the first seeds of perhaps healing for the tormented character Selma portrayed.

Director and Director of Photography

Director and DP collaboration is one of the most fertile, stimulating, and inspiring phases of prepping a movie. The DP, as a storyteller, will have great input into how to tell a story visually. As a director, I would watch many movies with the DP and look at different artists, still photography, paintings, and architecture books to get inspired and to share our vision.

We would spend hours and hours together over lunches and dinners, discussing every scene, every moment in the movie, all to create the movie's look and language. Discussions surround color palettes, atmosphere, lighting, camera movement, camera angles, transitional shots, lenses, and frame ratio all while creating a detailed shot list for every scene. There are no arbitrary angles or camera movements. They are all designed to best serve the story, its vision, and its intent.

The director and DP will also create a wish list for special equipment or accommodations such as a dolly, crane, drone, motion control, Steadicam, days with multi-cameras, insert cars for driving scenes, etc. The shot list will be discussed with all other heads of departments to collaborate on the designs and the DP needs for each scene. The AD will then have to translate the shot list to determine how much time to allocate for each scene in the schedule.

Storyboarding can be an important tool for complicated scenes. The storyboard will help all the creatives on set know what they need to do for a particular scene.

During filming, under time pressure, you may need to trim the shot list, and so it is smart to highlight which shots you absolutely need to tell the story. And last, be prepared to take the shot list and throw it out the window. As you see the walk-through of the actors on set, you might get inspired and want to change the choreography as well as the camera angles and shots.

Production Design

At AFI, I was lucky to have taken classes from the legendary Robert F. Boyle, who was Hitchcock's regular production designer. Bob opened our minds to the infinite possibilities of telling a story through the design of the sets. The wall colors, the furniture, the practical lights, the choice of locations, the matte paintings (the painted huge backgrounds that can be created digitally today), which extend the sets and create the illusion that you are in whatever location you choose, and the special, specific props all support the vision.

The production designer works closely with the director and the director of photography to define the look of the movie, the color palettes, the style, and the atmosphere. They also collaborate with the location manager to find the perfect locations to film. The designer will then bring on their team, including the art director, set dressers, shoppers, and builders to make the vision come to life.

The props master, the special effects supervisor, the armorer, set designer and dresser, the graphic designer, construction department, VFX (visual effects) and CGI (computer generated imagery) are all under the leadership of the production designer.

❀ *On Jungle, we had several flashback scenes that needed to take place in Israel, and I really wanted to film there. However, the schedule and budget didn't allow for such travel, so our Production Designer, Matt Putland, built Yossi's parents' traditional living room, a replica of an ancient courtyard from Jerusalem, and the facade of the Israeli Airport in the 80's. He also built an American diner. All was staged side by side in a huge warehouse, and we filmed those scenes quickly and economically.*

Costume Design

For an actor, embracing their character often begins with the costume. They can fully morph into the role as they put on their wardrobe. They have great instincts about what works for them and what doesn't.

The costume designer will create a mood board and come up with ideas for a specific look for each character. They will also make their own breakdowns and mark all their costumes per the script's progression and each character's changes. In designing the costumes, they will take into consideration things like the need to hide knee pads, straps, and other safety gear as well as the need to have doubles, triples, or more of the same costumes for the doubles and stunt performers, or if a certain wardrobe will be ruined in a scene. Other things to consider are the weather, continuity, special costumes or uniforms for period and sci-fi movies.

Costume rental houses could supply many of the costumes, but often the designer will need to produce the wardrobe per the script needs.

When I prep for directing, I often look at fashion magazines for inspiration as to how the characters will look. Of course, the designer will bring their own ideas, which often exceed my imagination and contribute to deepening the character and their backstory.

The costume department will usually include the costume designer, costumer, seamstress, shopper, and on-set costumer who can make adjustments as needed to ensure the costume looks good on the actor while filming.

❀ *During a fitting session for* A Thousand Kisses Deep, *the amazingly talented and one of the most gracious actors you will ever meet, Dougray Scott loved a hat the costume designer presented to him. I wasn't sold on it as it would be challenging for lighting and camera angles, but Dougray insisted. And he was right. The hat allowed him to bring another layer to the character that had not been written in the script. He was telling a story with the hat. In a scene, where his wife confronted him about his whereabouts suspecting he had cheated on her, he needed to come up with a good lie on the spot. So he took a deep breath, slowly took off the hat and placed it on the bar counter, he then fixed his hair and only then replied to his wife. The hat and all the activity around it allowed him time to create a new level of subtext within the scene. You could almost "see" how his brain worked during those moments.*

When talking with actors about their wardrobe or when visiting a fitting session, it is important to be patient, sensitive, and aware of what you say. On a movie I directed, the actress and I came up with a specific look for her where she would mostly wear a tight, black, cigarette skirt. We both loved the look and matched it with fabulous different tops. We then showed one of the male producers pictures from the fitting session. He looked at the actress and told her the skirt made her hips look big. Ahhhh, oy-vey, silent, and before I could say anything, that young sharp actress just looked him in the eye and replied, "And what is wrong with that?" The producer tried to mumble something, and we never got another wardrobe note from him.

Hair and Makeup Department

Hair and makeup are crucial elements that contribute to the movie's overall look and help the cast members start building their characters. The director will share their vision with the hair and makeup artists, who will then bring that vision to life. Sometimes prosthetics artists will join the team to create a specific look for the actor. The special effects makeup must be designed and fitted specifically to an actor, including scars, tattoos, wounds, noses, double chin, bald heads and sometimes a full-facial mask.

The hair and makeup department usually includes the main hair stylist and makeup artist. They will be the ones designing the look and will usually stay in the makeup and hair trailer to work with the actors. They will each have other makeup and hair stylists working depending on the size of the cast. Sometimes extra help will be booked only for days with a large number of actors and background artists. They will also have a hair stylist and makeup artist on set to adjust between takes.

The AD accounts for time to get actors through hair and makeup first thing in the morning. This may sometimes require a precall for that department and the actors, and as a consequence, to the location manager and transportation department to get the trailers ready. Enough time should also be allocated for changes between scenes and the different looks. The hair and makeup trailer is like a shrine where transformations happen, and characters are born. Some actors may want quiet time to concentrate before their scenes, some may use their time on the chair to read their lines, and some may feel chatty. Hair and makeup artists are usually very sensitive and attentive to the cast needs.

Wigs, mustaches, beards, nail treatments, facial prosthetics applications to change someone's look, and spray tanning, all count under the hair and makeup department collaborating with special effects makeup and designers.

✾ *One of the most iconic moments in Jungle, is when Daniel Radcliffe feels that something is moving inside a huge bump on his forehead. With a pair of tweezers, he cuts the bump, and a gush of blood squirts out of it along with a long twirly worm. The special effects makeup artist built the huge bump and applied it on Daniel's forehead filled with fake blood and a fake long worm made from some gooey material you make gummy bears from. In postproduction we added the worm's movement under the skin. We only shot a real live worm in the bucket where Daniel collected the fake blood and anything else that came out of that bump.*

Transportation

The Transportation Department carries the weight of the entire production. Drivers are usually the first to arrive on set and the last to leave. They are the pillars of base camp operations, moving trucks and trailers from location to location, ensuring everything is in working order and that fuel levels, including those for generators, are sufficient. At the start of the day, they prepare and maintain the trailers, ensuring that toilets and sinks have running water and that air conditioning or heaters are turned on as needed. Even a single delay in the arrival of an equipment truck can disrupt the whole production, so they take extra precautions to be prepared for unexpected traffic, flat tires, or other challenges.

The head of the department is the transportation coordinator, and the second in command is the Captain. The two will hire the drivers and will arrange for the rental of all the trucks and trailers. They will also work closely with the location manager and the first AD on where to set up the "base camp," parking for the crew, coordinating shuttles for the cast and crew to set and, if filming on remote location, pick up and drop off for the leading cast from their hotel to set and back.

A basic low-budget package includes:

- Eight-room honey wagon with private toilets to accommodate the cast
- Three-room trailer—a trailer with three spacious well-equipped rooms usually given to the main stars and the director
- Hair/makeup and wardrobe combo trailer
- Camera truck
- Grip truck

- Electric truck
- Props truck
- Art truck
- Location truck with safety cones, vests, heaters, coolers, directors' chairs, base camp tents, and chairs
- Catering truck and craft service vehicle
- Stakebeds for towing the trailers and to help with short-distance company moves
- Gas tanker to refuel the trucks if you are in a remote location
- Water truck to wet floor for look if needed but also may be required by the permit office for safety in fire-prone locations
- Generator to give power to both the base camp as well as the set lights
- Toilets if needed in addition to the honey wagon

It is important during prep to discuss where all these trucks will be parked so they are far enough away from the set not to interrupt the filming or appear in the shot but close enough that you don't waste time shuttling cast and crew back and forth, if possible.

Picture Cars

Picture cars are the vehicles that will be shown on camera. Picture car rental companies can generally provide any vehicle you may need, including police cars, ambulances, buses, fire trucks, exotic cars, period rare cars, etc. The prop department will add the appropriate license plate based on where the movie is set as well as any interior props. Try to schedule picture car scenes sequentially to save on rentals.

If you need to crash or otherwise destroy a car, you must purchase the picture car. You may even need to buy several for multiple takes or if you are not filming in script order.

Always have a mechanic check the picture car, and be sure to have any vintage cars towed, rather than driven, to location.

If you're using a picture car, you will oftentimes need to rent an insert car to carry the picture car and crew so the actor doesn't have to actually drive and cameras and lights can be positioned on the loading ramp. The car can also have a crane, which is perfect for chase scenes.

❀ *On the movie* The Frontier, *we had a few gorgeous vintage cars that we rented. They were older and not in great shape mechanically. Per the rental agreement, we towed them to the isolated diner set, Club Ed, in Lancaster, California. But when it was time to film the car during magic hour, it wouldn't start. We were losing the light and the shot had to be done within the next fifteen minutes, or we wouldn't get it. Luckily on this one, we planned well, and one of the teamsters was a mechanic. He jumped in, turned some knobs, and the car was ready to drive. We were able to continue shooting with the stunning desert sunset.*

Catering and Craft Services

Feed your crew well!

Shooting days are long, and the cast and crew work constantly with a very high level of concentration and focus in every department. The production company tries to accommodate the crew's needs to make their experience as comfortable as possible so they can concentrate on the work. It is important to be nourished with healthy, fresh, and cooked food.

During prep you will hire the catering company. Oftentimes chefs will come and do a huge spread for the production office to "audition," and everyone gets to have a little preproduction party and a vote.

You should hire a catering service that specializes in movie productions. They understand the specific needs of a crew and movie schedules. When call time is at night for an all-night shoot, we still call the first meal breakfast and at 2 a.m., lunch... that's the movie life. There should always be enough options for dietary restrictions, preferences and/or allergies, vegan, and vegetarian options. Lunch time is a sacred time for everyone to unwind, make some private calls, and even take power naps. Also during this time, the director, producer, and first AD, often confer on the next day's plans and call sheet or whatever else needs to be decided.

The catering service along with the location department will arrange for tables and chairs and find a proper area to host the large crew.

There is a strict rule that everyone needs to have a hot, seated meal six hours from call time. Then six hours later, if you have not yet wrapped, you must provide a second meal. The time for lunch, whether it is half an hour or an hour, will be calculated from the time the last person on the crew passes through the line.

Grace

If lunch is called after the six-hour mark, you can call for "grace" if the lens has not changed and if the shot is exactly the same, which means you'll be able to continue filming without paying a penalty.

Penalty

On the rare occasion where you choose to continue filming beyond grace—perhaps to get the proper light, for weather concerns, or to accommodate an actor's schedule—the production will have to pay a penalty to all the crew and actors who are on set and have not broken for lunch.

On some occasions might consider "French Hours," which means the cast and crew will have the food available over a few hours instead of having an official seated lunch or dinner time. Everyone takes turns eating while the rest keep working. This means that wrap time will be an hour earlier and the day as a whole will be shorter. This is often used when filming takes place during winter when the days are short and the sun sets too early. This way you don't waste an hour of precious daylight sitting and eating, and you can maximize the shooting hours.

Craft Service

The craft service table will be set up all day serving coffee, tea, healthy (and sometimes not-so-healthy) snacks, warm soup in winter or popsicles in summer. Make it fun for your crew! It's always nice to add some vitamins, sanitary napkins, sunscreen, and other daily perks.

Music Clearance

When filming a scene where the actors are performing a song on camera, you will need to clear the rights during prep as once the scene is shot, you will not be able to replace the song. The rights to clear are:

- **Publishing rights:** are the rights associated with the composition (lyrics and melody), which are typically controlled by a publishing company with whom you will need to negotiate licensing the rights.

- **Master rights:** refers to the actual sound recording of a specific artist or band. Those rights are often controlled by the artist or their record label.

You can also choose precleared tracks from a music library, such as APM, one of the biggest libraries in the world, all the rights you need can be cleared in one stop. Or explore music in the public domain which is free of copyright restrictions.

Either way, you should always consult with a music supervisor or your lawyer to navigate those negotiations and clearance of rights.

❈ *While directing* Confessions of a Sociopathic Social Climber, *I was driving with my kids, listening to Billy Idol. My husband, Tal, played with him for years. When "Dancing with Myself" came on, and an idea was sparked in my mind. I imagined an opening montage of Jennifer Love Hewitt getting dressed, putting on makeup, getting ready for a night out, dancing to the song.*

The producers tried to get the master rights along with the publishing rights, but it was out of our budget. Instead, we secured the publishing rights and had Jennifer Love Hewitt record her version. It was about half the price of the master. We did however to use Billy Idol's original master for the trailer to attract viewers.

Editing Set Up

Here comes another storyteller—the editor. I love talking with the editor prior to making the movie in order to hear their thoughts about the script. A good editor will provide you with insights and suggestions about transitions and coverage that you may not have thought of. They also have great instincts about actor's performances, and I like to include them in my casting decisions.

The editor should begin editing from the first day of filming. They will carefully watch the dailies and start their assembly. This is important so they can provide valuable notes on coverage, performances, understanding of the location's geography, and orientation. If anything isn't working, the editor can flag it early, allowing time for the production to make adjustments. The editors will also highlight any technical issues and, most importantly, create an ongoing list of missing or needed shots—ensuring that everything essential is captured while locations, actors, wardrobe, and equipment are still available.

As long as you can set up a way to stream to the editor, the editor can work remotely and need not be on set. Remote editing has become standard practice, and plenty of programs enable this.

Scouting with the Crew

During the last week of prep, two or even three full days should be dedicated for the final scouting of all the filming locations.

The transportation department will arrange for either a big party bus or a couple of vans to accommodate most heads of departments (HOD's) and their second in command, (best boys) along with the director, producer, line producer, assistant director, and location manager, so everyone can discuss the final preparations and filming plans.

The director of photography and his gaffer and key grip will discuss all the necessary setups and any extra equipment. The production designer and set dresser will discuss the final details of the set decoration and approve it with the director. The assistant director will discuss with all department heads how long they would need to prep all locations and how long to wrap out of each location.

The transportation coordinator and the captain, will make final decisions as to where they should set up "base camp" and where the trucks, crew, and cast should park in each location. This is more important than you think. I once arrived to set and was horrified to see all the huge trucks parked outside the window of the set even though the shot list indicated we would be shooting through that window. It took us two hours to move them all so we could start filming the way the director planned with shots looking out to the gorgeous tree-lined street.

This time spent together with all HOD'S and technical crew allows for many practicall and creative conversations, which prepare everyone for the big production meeting.

Camera Test Day

A few days before filming, the camera team will prep the cameras, lenses, and monitors. They will test and check all the gear to make sure everything works in sync. During that day, the DP will set up the LUT (lookup table), which is a filter that can be applied to the monitors on set and embedded into the dailies so everyone can see the desired color palette and the style the DP is designing for the final coloring of the movie.

That day is also a good time to see the lead actors on camera with their hair, makeup, and wardrobe while the director is present and there is still time to allow for adjustments.

The first AD runs the day as if it's a mini shoot. It's also a good time to see everyone working together and time how long specific hair and makeup takes as well as how long it takes to change looks.

The Production Office

One of the most enjoyable and satisfying parts of making a movie is the collaboration between all the departments. The whole team works together toward one goal—make the best movie possible that is greater than the sum of its parts. This is why even on these days of remote working, a production team should always have a production office where each department is accessible and everyone can meet in person. Throughout prep and the shoot, all the heads of departments should be in constant communication and be aware of each other's choices. The production office will be the hub for a few more essential roles.

The production manager works closely with the line producer and will be responsible for hiring the main below-the-line crew and support teams. They will work closely with the location manager to make sure all permits are issued and paid. They will set up the accounts along with the accountant in all the rental houses. They do everything.

The production coordinator is the production's pillar. You can't survive a moment without them. They are the masters of the production office. They will handle the travel arrangements for cast and crew. They will follow up with lawyers on the work visas. They will ensure all office supplies are available, including the printer and they will not forget the snacks. During filming in collaboration with the AD's they will distribute the call sheet and help coordinate communication between the set and the editing room, etc.

And don't forget the PAs (production assistants). PAs are essential for a smooth running set and the production in general. You hope to hire eager assistants who want to learn and see that work as a way to get into the film business. Their job is basically doing anything that needs to be done. Treat them well. They work harder than anyone and, oftentimes, don't receive much gratitude.

Day out of Days and Schedule Sample

9:15 AM Day Out of Days Report for Cast Members

		Month/Day	11/07	11/08	11/09	11/10	11/11	11/12
		Day of Week	Mon	Tue	Wed	Thu	Fri	Sat
		Shooting Day	1	2	3	4	5	
1.	MARIA/AIRAM		SW	W	W		W	
2.	AMY			SW	W	W		
4.	DAN		SW	W	W	W	W	
3.	GINA							
5.	SEAN							
6.	MARK						SW	
7.	CLAUDIA		SW	W	WF			
8.	NAOMI		SW	W	WF			
9.	GABRIELLE							
10.	AARON							
11.	YOUNG WOMAN		SWF					
12.	DOCTOR					SWF		
13.	PRIEST							
15.	HOCKEY PLAYER							
14.	SECOND HOCKEY PLAYER							
16.	WAITER						SWF	

Sheet #:	Scenes:					Script Day
1 / 1 pgs	1	EXT / Morning	ROUTE 66 - THE FRONTIER / In the parking lot of The Frontier, LAINE meets LUANNE		1, 2	D1
7 / 3 pgs	7	EXT / Day	FRONTIER / CAFE / OFFICER GAULT helps LAINE with her tire		1, 2, 7	D1
12 / 1 5/8 pgs	11	EXT / Day	FRONTIER / CAFE / LAINE turns down LUANNE's job offer		1, 2, 7	D1
9 / 1/8 pgs	8A	INT/EXT / Day	CAFE / LAINE'S POV - LUANNE speaks to OFFICER GAULT		1, 2, 7	D1
8 / 1/8 pgs	8	INT/EXT / Day	CAFE / LAINE enters the cafe and peers out the window		1	D1
End of Shooting Day 1 -- Saturday, January 11, 2014 -- 5 7/8 Pages						
27 / 8 3/8 pgs	23	INT / Day	CAFE / LUANNE gives LAINE a job; GLORIA tells them her necklace was stolen		1, 2, 3, 4, 5, 7	D2
29 / 1/8 pgs	24A	INT/EXT / Day	FRONTIER / CAFE / GAULT'S POV - GAULT watches LAINE inside the cafe		1, 7	D2
End of Shooting Day 2 -- Sunday, January 12, 2014 -- 8 4/8 Pages						
3 / 2 6/8 pgs	3	INT / Morning	CAFE / LUANNE gives LAINE breakfast, offers her a shower; LEE enters		1, 2, 3	D1
10 / 1/8 pgs	9	INT / Day	CAFE / LAINE makes eye contact with LEE		1, 3	D1
11 / 3/8 pgs	10	INT / Day	CAFE - KITCHEN / LAINE grabs a cup; LEE blocks her way		1, 3	D1

Production Meeting

A few days prior to filming, the first AD will run the big production meeting. All HODs will attend along with the director and producers. In the meeting, the AD will go through the schedule per the breakdown, and everyone will ask questions. During this meeting, you won't be able to resolve all the issues that come up, but you'll be able to identify them and set up side-bar meetings afterward.

This meeting can take more than two days, but you can't skip it.

Usually in a production office you'll have to dedicate rooms to the director, the producer, the line producer, the production manager, the production coordinator with the PAs and/or assistant coordinator. Also you need rooms for the AD, accountant, DP, PD, props, wardrobe, transportation, and set dressing.

Go Green…

And a reminder, when you plan your project GO GREEN!!! Not only will you help save the planet, but you could potentially tap into some grants and other helpful resources. Check out the Green Production Guide which can provide you with the full "toolkit" if you are in the U.S, Albert for the UK and Green Film School Alliance if you are a student/short or indie filmmaker.

And off you go. Over the next couple of days, all the departments will check out and load their equipment onto the trucks, and the director will meet with actors and do final rehearsals and costume fittings. It will be the last weekend to relax, but you won't because you'll be excited and nervous and full of creative energy before you set off to film.

PART FOUR
FINALLY FILMING

A Dream Comes True.

The Call Sheet

Safety

Camera Department

Lighting

Grip Department

Props

Armorer

Special Effects

Construction Department

Stunts

Directing Actors

Sound

Green Screen & Virtual Productions

Background Actors

Script Supervisor

Filming Intimate Scenes

Child Actors – Minor Labor Rules

Security

Dailies

Problem Solving–You Plan, God Laughs

Electronic Press Kit

It's a Wrap

A Dream Comes True

That moment when you arrive on set for the first day of principal photography is a feeling I can't explain. After months of preparation, sometimes many years of development, and even more years of thinking about that story you want to tell, you are finally standing there with all those people who believed in your vision and are ready to work together to bring your dream to life.

And now it's really time to take the plunge!

The filming period is so intense, and every minute counts. Many elements, people, equipment, and moving parts have to work in harmony, and everyone's concentration level is at max for most of the day. In this chapter, I will introduce the main departments and roles of the key crew, which will be crucial in making the movie. This by no means covers everyone, but it will give you an idea as to what each department does. Naturally, although I mention them here in the filming chapter, they are all also busy during preproduction to prep for the moment on set, which is show time.

A lot is at stake, and so many things can go wrong, but try to be relaxed. If you prepped well, you are ready. Be creative and open minded to handle any challenge that might arise. Try to sleep and eat well, and be a positive leader on the set, it's contagious. Hurray, filming has begun!

The Call Sheet

The call sheet is a document issued at the end of each filming day by the AD department, that contains all the necessary information for everyone working on the movie for the following day. The call sheet, includes the call times for everyone, (different call times may be required for the different departments), the location addresses, what scenes will be shot, and in what order they will be filmed. It will also include contact information for everyone.

The call sheet will have other details from the breakdown pages, including how many background actors will arrive, what major props, stunts, picture cars, any special effects, or wardrobe needs, and any other important details about the day. It will state what time is lunch break and for the caterer, how many meals should be prepared. On the top of the page you will also find the weather prediction, the address for the closest hospital and any other special safety advisory. The call sheet will also include information on another day or two in advance so everyone can be reminded of what needs to be prepared.

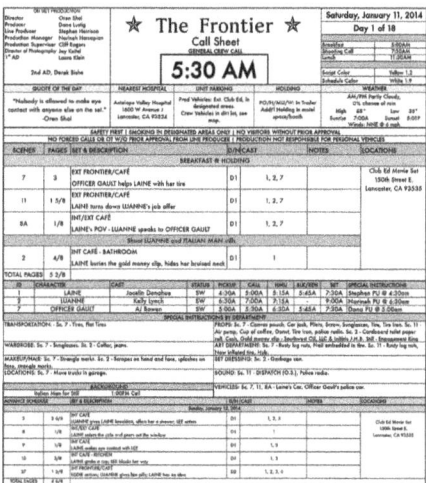

Safety

A film set can be a dangerous place. Each day should begin with the first AD gathering the crew for a safety meeting, covering any specific hazards for that day and location. Always secure permits and disclose your filming plans. The permit office can often alert you to potential risks and offer precautionary recommendations to keep everyone safe.

Make sure to have a medic on set for most days and for more challenging days, an ambulance should be standing by, especially when performing dangerous stunts. A fire marshal and a fire truck may be required in certain locations as well.

❀ *On my first movie as a PA, which starred James Earl Jones, I helped the special effects (SPEFX) person light a bonfire. He ran a long pipe from the propane tank, which ended under the fake wood where I stood with the lighter. When he told me to ignite it, a huge flame shot up, burning my bangs, eyebrows and eyelashes. I managed to put the flames out with my hands, and I'll never forget the sight of the Oscar-winning DP Mauro Fiore, the gaffer on that movie, who jumped from a high scaffold and ran over to cover me with a sound blanket. The careless SPEFX person had turned the propane tank on prematurely causing a pool of flammable propane in the area. He paid for my haircut, and I decided not to create any trouble for him. However, I learned to always hire top professionals when it comes to anything that has to do with safety.*

Camera Department

- **The Camera Operator:** Operating the camera requires precision, high focus, technical ability, and top physical shape but mostly fast instincts, a deep understanding of the story, and a high level of collaboration with the actors. The best operators are completely in tune with the actors performance and can adjust in real time the framing and movement of the camera.

  The director and the DP will discuss with the operator the opening and closing frames, and main focus of the specific shot. The operator will study the dialogue carefully so they can follow the actors performance, yet they are always ready for any improvisational moments during the take, to adjust the frame and capture the magic.

  Often times on lower-budget movies, the DP will also operate the camera. This is also the case when the style of filming may demand it. On union shows, a special waiver is needed to have the DP operate instead of hiring an operator.

- **The Focus Puller, or First AC, (Camera Assistant):** adjusts the focus, manually or by remote control. They will measure the distances between the camera and the actor or the subject being filmed and calculate how to pull focus even when the camera is moving. The focus puller will also study the scene to know which elements to focus on or wrack focus from, for instance, from one actor to another.

- **The Second AC:** is responsible for handling the camera lenses. They also handle all the camera cards (or film magazines if shooting on film).

- **DIT, the Digital Imaging Technician:** will create dailies and then store the data safely and prepare it to be transferred to a postproduction facility.

Lighting

Lighting is an art and is an integral part of telling the story and fostering the vision of the movie. Lights are part of the paint and brushes of the DP. The DP works closely with the gaffer, the chief lighting technician of the movie, to find the best way to achieve the look the director and DP carefully designed.

The lighting department consists of the gaffer, the best boy, who is responsible for the storage of all the equipment on the truck and the maintenance, and electricians, who rig the lights on set along with the grips. The genie operator is responsible for operating the generator.

The lighting setup can be huge and elaborate or minimal, depending on the location, the style of the movie, and the budget. Each light has a specific role in creating the atmosphere and look of the scene. The lights can soften and complement an actor's face to make them look glamorous, or they can make them look malicious and scary. The lights can emulate moonlight or sun rays coming through a window or reflected in a water source. Lighting can call attention to where the action is or to some detail on which the director wants the audience to focus.

In addition, practical lights on the set, such as lamps, chandeliers, streetlights, neon signs, fridge lights, car headlights, cell phones, and any other light source can become part of the set design, and lighting design and can be used to create an atmosphere. Natural light can be manipulated with reflectors, flags, and silk frames.

❀ *By using practical lights and light beaming in through windows, the brilliantly talented DP and nicest person, Pedro Luque, on* Look Away, *left the set largely free of light stands. This gave the actors and the camera the freedom to move around.*

For example, his lighting of a particular scene through tree branches contributed to the terrifying atmosphere, creating scary shadows as India Eisley, the gifted actress, walked at night alone in the corridor.

Pedro has the talent to take any location, as naked as it may be (e.g., an ice-skating rink with flat fluorescent lights), and turn it into a stunning location. When India walked onto the ice to face some of her classmates during their prom, the camera was set behind her. Pedro placed a bright light in front of her, and we had her walk toward it. All you could see was her silhouette and reflections of her sparkly dress.

The lighting, camera movement, and angle, worked together to tell the story of an excited but scared girl walking bravely into a trap during the prom. The atmosphere allowed the audience to anticipate the disaster that was about to happen.

During an exterior night shoot on Kill Me Later, *we ran out of time to light a scene. With the sun coming up, DP David Ferrara was hesitant to shoot, and we almost gave up on filming. However, in the moment, it was a matter of filming with compromised lighting or not getting the scene at all. As the director, I knew I needed the scene, so we improvised and shot the scene using car headlights.*

Grip Department

The grip department is assembled from a team of experienced, resourceful crew members who have very specific, important roles in the whole running of the set. They work closely with the DP, lighting, and camera departments. They assemble and rig all the support equipment for the lighting and camera department. They build and set up the means to hang lights and lamps, whether on stands, built scaffolding, or hanging rods.

They will assemble huge reflectors, flags, and silks to cut the light, direct it into a specific spot, or defuse it. They will secure the stands and lights with sandbags and ropes. The grip department will also assemble the tracks for the dolly, and they will operate the various cranes. Often, the grip department will ask for prep days at a certain location to rig equipment and save time on the day of filming.

The key grip is the head of the department and will work closely with the DP and the gaffer during prep to design and prepare for all the set's needs.

The dolly grip studies the scene ahead of time to stay in tune with the actors' rhythm and the camera operator's movements as they roll the dolly. They remain highly attentive to all elements happening simultaneously and try to adjust their pace in real-time as the scene unfolds.

The best boy grip has many responsibilities including checking out, taking care and organizing of all equipment on the truck.

The department may also have other grips working, depending on the size of the production.

Props

Props are objects or items the actors might use during filming. Anything they touch becomes a prop—from cigarettes to rosaries, wallets, watches, sunglasses, money, food, and any specific artifact that might be needed for the scene. The prop master will collect or manufacture the props and will invite the director for show-and-tell sessions where they present the props and receive notes or approval.

Actors love props as they can find other layers of their characters, and so much can be told about a character based on their usage of props. A great actor can build an entire moment around a specific prop.

❀ During my first director's meeting with actor Rob Schneider for the movie Wild Cherry, *he said he would love to accept the offer if we could work on some of his scenes and rewrite them together. With Rob's massive experience with comedy, Chris Charney, the screenwriter and I, welcomed the idea. And so, for about a week, I would drive over to Rob's house in Pasadena while Chris was in Canada, and we would sit until the wee hours of the night rewriting.*

In one of the scenes, Rob's character, a single father, is supposed to lecture his teen-age daughter, Tanya Raymond, on how to use contraceptives, and we were looking for a way to elevate the comedy. Not sure how to achieve this but hoping to spark an idea, I went to the pharmacy and bought every contraceptive they had. My husband seriously wondered what was going on, but Rob was inspired. We then rewrote that scene and Rob had a field day demonstrating every single one of them for his mortified daughter. The contraceptive props, Rob's straight performance, and Tanya's embarrassed reaction made the scene come to life.

Armorer

A professional and licensed armorer handles firearms on set—pistols, rifles, shotguns, machine guns, and submachine guns—as well as historical firearms like flintlocks and percussion caps.

Often, actors undergo basic training during prep to know how to handle weapons.

These days, for safety reasons, the tendency is to simulate muzzle flash in CGI during post-production, and many precautionary procedures are required during filming for those who still use real firearms on set.

Shooting blanks: A blank cartridge is used in real firearms and has a cartridge case with gunpowder but no bullet, so it doesn't shoot a projectile. However, it still produces smoke, a flash, and a loud bang. This means that even blanks can be dangerous at close range due to the force and gases released.

A dummy round inserted into the weapon looks completely real, but it can't be fired. It has no gunpowder, and it won't produce flash or sound. It is completely safe. The danger with dummy bullets is that they look so real that if someone is not careful, they can be confused or mixed with the real ones.

On prop guns the barrel is smaller and won't allow a bullet to be fired from them. They only produce smoke and sound. Rubber guns also look great but will require a VFX spark to be added in postproduction just as guns with a blocked barrel do.

Squibs create the effect of a bullet hit. You rig the equipment on the actor, or wherever you want to show the bullet hit, and it is then operated remotely with a detonator. This is usually handled by the special effects expert on set.

Special Effects

The special effects department (SEFX) is responsible for building and operating all practical effects on set, as opposed to visual effects (VFX), which are digitally created in postproduction.

The SEFX artists will create and operate the rain, snow, wind, smoke and fog machines. As well as designing, reimagining and manufacturing ways to create events such as sandstorms, earthquakes, explosions, fires, floods and any other catastrophe or magical moment the script may call for. Within their department, they will build creatures and animals from various materials to make them look and feel creepily real. They will closely work with the props department as the cast will often handle those creations. The SEFX artists will also collaborate with the stunt department, construction crew, and grips to handle chase scenes, car accidents, flat tires, flipped cars and explosions.

❁ *The SEFX department on* Jungle *had to create a huge, scary snake, make a fake slimy chicken embryo, dig and put together a fake quicksand pool for Daniel to almost drown in, create a major rainstorm that would last for hours over a large rocky jungle area, construct several rafts for the rough waters, which needed to crash and land on a fake planted rock in the middle of the river, and much more.*

One of my favorite scenes in Jungle *is when the three friends and their guide are sitting around a campfire eating a monkey they hunted. The SEFX department created a burned monkey (actually, a few of them for retakes). It looked so real and scary. The cast ripped the monkey apart, chewing the legs and arms. The cherry on top was the white, mushy brain enjoyed by the creepy character Karl, played by Thomas Kretschmann.*

I love the scene, not only because of its gory quality but because the character of each of the friends and the dynamics among them is revealed and changed. With only two lines, the scene is purely visual. We realized that poor Marcus, played by Joel Jackson, was not equipped to be on this journey while Yossi, played by Radcliffe, and Kevin, played by Alex Russell, had immersed themselves in the adventure, and the only person who actually took care of Joel was Kretschmann's character with one simple line: "I'll make you some rice."

Construction Department

The construction department could be responsible for building an entire city or just a tiny closet. The script and the budget dictate how large this department will be. It includes welders, carpenters, painters and any other skilled labor that is required.

❀ On Breakwater, *masterly directed by James Rowe, the script called for a hidden, isolated wooden shack placed on the bank of a marsh, which you could only access with a little boat. We scouted for weeks to find this location, and when we couldn't, the production designer and his team built one on a floating ramp, which we could then tow to a spectacular location in the middle of an alligator-infested marsh. We then had to shuttle Dermot Mulroney and the five-year-old Ezra DuVall, as well as the crew, back and forth on little motorboats to shoot. It was difficult and a bit scary, but the scene is incredibly gorgeous and unique.*

Stunts

It is always exciting to work with the stunt coordinator and their team to create innovative and thrilling moments. They will always try to push the envelope and develop never-before-seen fights, jumps, chases, falls, and car flips.

Stunt performers, working under SAG contracts, are cast by a stunt coordinator based on both physical resemblance to the actor and their specialized skills. Any stunt that is planned needs to be disclosed to the insurance company and they will usually charge for the extra risk. The permit office will also analyze the risks and the needed accommodations including police units to block streets, fire marshals for any shooting or other fire hazards, and definitely medical teams including an ambulance standing by on set.

❀ *My tensest moment on set was during the filming of Jungle on a whitewater river in the middle of Colombia. We were filming two stunt performers on a raft. Thirty meters before a major, dangerous waterfall, they were supposed to veer toward the riverbank where pickup trucks and many grips were waiting to carry them off the water and drive them back upriver for another take. However, we were running a half hour later than planned that day and because of this, the tide began to rise and the current became rougher by the minute.*

The stunt performers lost control, and the raft began to drift toward the falls, and they were suddenly in real danger. I stood on the riverbank terrified along with the other 150 people on the crew. We had no way to help them. Disaster was looming. But then, like two angels from heaven, local stunt performers on each side of the river, both expert kayakers, jumped into their kayaks just ahead of the raft and managed to block the raft from reaching the falls. They steered the raft to safety among much cheering and sighs of relief. Many quiet prayers were said that night.

Directing Actors

As a director, I like to meet with the actors prior to filming to talk about the characters, their backstory, their relationship with other characters, and their arc. It is also the time when we get to know each other, gain trust, and develop a sort of familiarity that will allow us later on set to recall things we talked about to help understand a specific moment in the script. I love to hear about actors' processes, what method of acting they like, and what they feel can help them perform best.

Some actors employ the method acting technique and practice sense memory while others may be more analytical, but they all thrive to make us, the audience, believe in the authenticity of what they say and how they behave. As a director, you can give ideas and precise direction, but ultimately you become a bit like the conductor and their musicians or a player and their coach. In the end, the player will need to perform on the court and the coach will be sitting on the sidelines hoping for the magic to happen.

Some actors love ad-libbing to bring their characters to life. Others stay true to the script. When I worked with the late Shakespearean actor David Warner, while directing *A Thousand Kisses Deep*, he asked for my permission to move a comma in a certain line to give the sentence a different read. This is how much he respected the written word and my vision as a director.

❀ *On a movie I produced, a notable actor, who sometimes stutters when he is off camera but never when he is performing, had a problem with one specific word in the middle of his monologue. The director kept cutting the take and had the actor start all over again. This happened a few times until the actor finally grew frustrated with a first-time director and demanded I direct the scene. It was during his final monologue of the film, right before we shot a big stunt, and everyone was on edge.*

Nothing I said calmed the actor down, and I realized I had to comply if we wanted to finish the filming what was planned for that night. The director reluctantly agreed to step aside for this one scene, and I took over. I briefly talked with the actor and called action. The actor did great until that specific word he had a problem with, and once again, he could not say it right and was ready to quit.

As the director had cut the take every time the actor arrived at that part, the actor and crew thought I would also cut. However, I called, "keep rolling" to the crew and to the actor. I told him I loved the performance and we'd cover that one part later and he should continue. He completed the monologue. I told him; it was perfect, and I asked him if he wanted another take.

He said yes. I knew he would, and off he went to perform the full monologue perfectly. All he needed was his director's trust, support, and love. He needed to feel secure to dare to take chances, to be in the moment knowing someone was carefully watching who wouldn't let him fail. I really didn't do much; it was all him, but my prior experience as an actor really helped me to understand his frame of mind.

We then moved on to film the stunt performer "falling" from the 13th floor backward onto a huge inflatable mattress on the ground. As it was a windy night, the stunt team threw sandbags weighing 200 pounds to see if they would land in the center of the mattress. Sometimes, they missed. I thought they would want to cancel the jump, but they didn't. We all stood nervously by the ambulance and police cars blocking traffic, and as the sun rose, the stunt performer finally jumped and did all kinds of maneuvers in the air; it was breathtaking. He landed safely, although not in the center, but his team was there to catch him. Everyone clapped as customary on movie sets, but people driving on the freeway started flooding 911 with calls reporting a jumper

Sound

Recording good quality dialogue is crucial. Without good sound, you may miss the authenticity and nuance within the performance. You may even need to ADR (additional dialogue replacement) the scene later in post.

The sound mixer should be well-versed in the locations so they can be ready for filming. Sound is usually recorded with one main mic held and directed by the boom operator. In addition, every actor usually has a lavalier microphone as well. The sound mixer will be by their recorder, monitoring the sound, and will ask to stop a take if they recognize issues. They use the assistance of the wardrobe person on set to figure out how best to fit each actor with their lav mic.

The costume designer will try to dress the actors with materials that do not cause too much sound and friction. Felt is often glued to the actor's shoes to avoid the sound of steps that could interrupt recording clean and usable dialogue.

The person holding the boom (boom operator) will also have to collaborate with the camera and figure out where to stand and how best to position the mic without causing shadows or entering the frame.

The Video Village

The video village is the area where a few monitors are set up so the director, DP, script supervisor and producers can watch what is being filmed. Extra monitors are set up for anyone else who needs to examine the frame closely while filming. As a director, once the shot and framing are set and all technical issues are discussed, I like to leave the monitor and get close to the actors to watch the performance live, not on the monitor. It's almost like I'm an actor in the scene. I get to feel the moment, be there with the actors, and know what adjustments should be made.

Green Screen and Virtual Productions

If your movie requires a lot of VFX shots—like fantastical, invented worlds or creatures—and requires very complicated filming or dangerous on-set situations, you always have the option to shoot in a studio in one of two techniques.

Green Screen

Filming actors and the practical set elements against a green screen, and then the background will be "keyed in" or added during postproduction. This method is very popular and relatively inexpensive, and has been used for many years.

Virtual Production

Virtual productions refers to the extraordinary newest technology where 3D images created in CGI prior to filming are displayed on huge LED panels that surround the set. In virtual production lingo, those massive sets are called the vault.

When using a set made out of LED walls, the on-set camera will be synced with the virtual camera so as the on-set camera moves, the virtual one can change the perspective, creating a parallax, which gives the feeling of realism. The virtual production helps actors' performances as they can react to the action projected rather than having to imagine it.

LED virtual productions are becoming more affordable, even for indie filmmakers. Filming on stage allows one to film magic hour scenes for as many hours a day as needed and move from a frozen or snowy environment to a hot desert within minutes. Coupled with an actual built set on the stage and costume changes, you can really go anywhere. The environment is controlled, and you don't need to worry about weather changes since you are in the studio.

Background Actors

Audiences don't always fully appreciate the work of background actors, but they fulfill an essential role on any movie set adding atmospheric realism to the scenes. I have lots of respect for the professionals who often bring their own wardrobe, do their own hair and makeup, and often are well-trained actors themselves.

The extra casting agencies will work closely with the first AD to cast the appropriate background actors for each scene per their ages, skills (e.g., do they need to be bodybuilders for a gym scene or ice skaters, etc.), and sometimes ethnicity. The extras agencies will also cast the stand-ins, background actors who resemble the leading actors in size and can double for them while the technical crew sets up the lights, etc., all while the cast is in the makeup and wardrobe trailers.

When accounting for catering, transportation, specialty wardrobe and even hair and makeup, having extras can be a very expensive ordeal. For scenes that in the past required hundreds or thousands of extras, such as sports stadiums, visual effects can be employed, greatly reducing the number of extras required. However, you will always need the real extras to perform and become an integral part of the scene.

The first AD usually directs the background action. If you choose to feature a background actor or give them a line, they will be upgraded to an actor role for the day, meaning they will receive a credit in the movie and an actor's day rate.

❀ *When filming in Colombia for* Jungle, *we had built a gorgeous indigenous village in the proximity of Bogota on a riverbank. Our extras casting director managed to bring background performers who still live in the rainforest to give the scenes in that village authenticity. I loved connecting with those gracious beautiful women, and we managed to communicate with each other, talking about motherhood and life even without understanding a word of each other's language.*

Script Supervisor

The script supervisor takes detailed notes during filming, capturing everything that happens on each take. They mark the director's favorite 'circled' takes, provide the correct scene number to be written on the slate, and follow the shot list to ensure nothing is missed. They also assist in discussions with the DP and director on-screen direction, the 180-degree rule, and actors' eyeline. These notes are crucial in editing. Additionally, they can "feed" actors with lines if any are forgotten.

The script supervisor is also responsible for ensuring continuity, or consistency, from one take to the next. If a glass in one take is half full, the script supervisor makes sure it isn't a quarter full in the next take. Film buffs get a kick out of identifying continuity errors in film, so this is a very important responsibility.

❀ *On* A Thousand Kisses Deep, *we shot a fight scene where Stuart Martin and Julian Rivett pull Dougray Scott and Jodie Whittaker into a car to collect a debt. As Dougray doesn't have the money, Julian hits him in the face. We shot a few takes where we would run the scene up to the hit and then stop for another take. Then, the makeup artist rushed in to apply the bleeding wound on Dougray and we continued to film the second part of the scene.*

Months later, in the editing room, the famous editor Humphrey Dixon (A Room with a View) and I never looked at one specific take, because the script supervisor noted that the bloody wound was not applied. It was the first take in which I did not want to stop the flow. But we were looking for a particular sentiment, and we decided to look at the shot anyway. It was the best by far. We used it, and if you look carefully at the scene, you'll see that there is one shot after Dougray was hit where there is no wound, yet the scene works great, and no one ever noticed. Sometimes performance supersedes continuity.

Filming Intimate Scenes

Some actors feel very comfortable performing intimate scenes while others are more reserved. This delicate issue needs to be discussed openly prior to production. The discussions between the director and the actor should be detailed and specific. It is important to discuss camera angles, wardrobe, what the actor feels comfortable with, and what might make them uncomfortable. It is important to note that some crew members may also feel awkward while filming those scenes, and extra consideration should be given to them as well.

A nudity waiver will need to be signed by the actor and producer prior to the day of filming, which will describe exactly what was agreed upon. When filming an intimate scene, it should be a closed set. No one should be there unless needed and an intimacy coordinator is always helpful facilitating the scene.

❀ I once worked with a young actress who, during rehearsals, realized that certain scenes were too risqué for her, and she requested that we cut those moments from the script. We were two weeks from filming, and I felt that the scenes were necessary the way they were. We, therefore, decided it would be better if we parted ways with the actress. I was grateful she was brave enough to bring up her concerns prior to filming to allow us time to recast. Recasting turned out to be the absolute correct decision.

On the same movie, I met with an actress in a fancy hotel lobby to talk about a different role, which also included an intimate scene. She was an amazing performer who treated her body as a vehicle for the role and had total dedication. When we discussed the scene and I asked her if she felt comfortable with the nudity, she offered to take off her shirt right there in the lobby to show me how comfortable she was. Naturally, I stopped her, she didn't, but it was an amazing experience working with her, and we choreographed a beautiful sensitive, touching, and funny scene together with the utmost respect and dignity for her, her partner, and the entire crew.

Child Actors–Minor Labor Rules

Children can steal any scene; however, you need to be aware of many protective union and labor laws. The AD will plan the schedule around the kid's availability as different ages have varying work hour limitations as well as rules regarding a parent's presence on set (stricter rules for younger children). You will also need to hire a set teacher to teach children during scheduled break times throughout the day.

That is why when having very young children on movie sets or TV shows, twins are often cast. This way you get double the number of hours you can shoot with the child during the day.

It is also important to discuss any explicit content with the parent before filming so they are comfortable with the material.

Signing contracts with minors is also a consideration. At the very least, you must get the signature of the parent. Sometimes when they get older, the child actors will challenge the validity of the contract, saying they were too young to know what they were signing and shouldn't be held to the terms. If that happens, you could have a problem. For that reason, many production companies go to the local court to have the contract ratified by a judge so the contract cannot later be challenged by the child.

Security

Hiring a security company is important to guard the sets, trucks, and equipment overnight or whenever you are filming in a place where the safety of your cast, crew, and equipment might be compromised.

Some actors have their own security team or bodyguards, which you might need to include as part of the budget, but it is necessary when an actor may have a stalker or threats to their safety. Most times, famous actors will use a pseudonym to register in the hotel and for the call sheet to avoid any inconveniences.

❀ *When filming in Colombia for Jungle, we had a lot of security concerns, especially regarding our star, Daniel Radcliffe. The Colombian government and film commissioners were very sensitive to our needs and provided ample security. They arranged armed vehicles, soldiers, security, and police cars. We arrived at a beautiful, remote village on a riverbank at the edge of the jungle, security in tow, vigilant to protect our actor. However, we noticed that the villagers were more intrigued by the drones and camera equipment, and no one was paying any attention to Daniel. It turns out that they did not watch movies and had no idea who Daniel Radcliffe was or even Harry Potter for that matter. From that moment on we let our guard down and enjoyed the tranquility of the location without worrying about our star.*

Dailies

Dailies used to be referred to as rushes, as film would have to be developed in a "rushed" manner at the lab to be screened at the end of the next shooting day. Today, since most movies and TV shows are shot digitally, it is customary to receive dailies as a protected link. There is still great benefit to watching dailies together as a production team because everyone can discuss whether they want to make adjustments on the following days to things like lighting, wardrobe, or performances. Sometimes, however, after the first few days, you will end up watching them on your computer as you're so exhausted after a long day of shooting.

If filming digitally, the process of getting dailies is as follows:

- The digital imaging technician (DIT) collects the cameras' original files and the sound recording throughout the day, verifying that all takes are accounted for, both sound and picture. The DIT creates two duplicate copies of the day's media to large hard drives or uploads to a virtual storage facility. The DIT syncs the sound to the picture, normalizes the color, and creates a proxy, which is a lower-resolution file for the editorial department.

- For security reasons, links to watermarked dailies are provided to a list of users approved by the producer, including the director, the DP, and other HOD'S.

- The assistant editor inputs the camera and sound original files into the editing system, so the editor can begin assembling a first cut during the shoot.

- Backup—have at least three copies of all footage in different locations. Ideally one of these will be cloud-based storage.

Problem Solving—You Plan, God Laughs

As a producer, no matter how well you've prepped, no matter how much experience you have, issues will always arise that you can never predict. At that point, your skill as a problem-solver will be necessary. You'll need to be fast and creative to find proper solutions. Thank goodness no one ever got terribly hurt on any of my shoots, but here are just a couple of examples of some unexpected situations.

❀ We had scouted all locations in Colombia for Jungle, including white water rivers, a few months prior to shooting. However, when we were all there getting ready for the shoot and we drove to the location on our tech scout, we were horrified to realize the river was dry. In fact, all the rivers around us were dry. This was terrible. So, we had a small plane fly us around above the dense jungles looking for white water rivers. We finally found one, but the whole process was very nerve-racking.

I produced Fauda's director, Assaf Bernstein's movie, Look Away in Winnipeg, Canada, where during the winter it is so cold that if you spill water, it will freeze in midair. We needed to film on a frozen lake for outdoor ice-skating scenes, but that specific winter, for the first time maybe ever, it didn't freeze or snow by Thanksgiving. We had to change the whole schedule and film the interiors first with fake snow on the windows while we waited for real snow and a frozen lake.

However, Oscar-winner Mira Sorvino, and remarkable Jason Isaacs were not in Winnipeg at the time. Luckily, they were available and could hop on the first plane out and be in the scenes. Then, one day, I opened the window in my hotel and the whole city was covered in white. Our prayers were answered, and we were finally able to shoot the outdoor scenes. Who said global warming is not real!

We shot The Frontier in Lancaster, California. Our costume designer used a local seamstress to take in a dress for the star, Kelly Lynch. Unfortunately, the day we *needed the dress, the shop was closed! We didn't have a backup, and without the dress, we would not have been able to shoot the day's scenes. Major crisis in the making!!!*

So, I called the local police, hoping they would know where the seamstress lived. She was woken up by two policemen and was immediately relieved to learn that all they were looking for was that dress. Problem solved and the director, Oren Shai, had no idea about the drama that was happening behind the scenes, and beautiful Kelly Lynch showed up in all her glory to set with the glamorous dress.

On the movie The Circle, *we shot in one continuous take for ninety minutes. Every night over one week, we filmed the whole movie with the intention of choosing the best take as the final picture. It was a very complicated production moving through numerous locations and setups. Around the middle of the movie, one scene takes place in a bar with an exotic dancer in the background.*

On the first night when we filmed the entire movie, about thirty minutes into the shot, we realized the dancer had not shown up. Having produced Dancing in the Blue Iguana, *just a couple of years earlier, I kind of knew a few moves and so I got on stage (fully clothed) and did some of the pole moves to the best to my ability. The look on the DP, director, and actors' faces, who knew nothing about the drama unfolding, was priceless. They were stunned but continued filming. In the end, a take from another night was chosen to be the final movie where we did have the real dancer on camera.*

I have had to move entire crews from their hotel due to bed bugs. I have had to fire people mid-production (not before I found a replacement). I have had actors missing planes. I have had a full day's filming lost due to technical difficulties. I have had so many problems on every film, but it's the nature of the job. However, I always remember, any day on a set is a miracle, and I stay grateful and never, ever, take the opportunity for granted.

Electronic Press Kit

During filming, you should plan to shoot some behind-the-scenes footage as well as lots of still photography (stills) so you can use it for publicity purposes when the movie is released. You should schedule your behind-the-scenes days on your most exciting filming days but also coordinate with your actors to make sure they are comfortable. Find times to get interviews with your lead actors, director, producer, and anyone else who might have an interesting story to tell.

In this day and age, it is also important to start making your social media presence felt. Create an account and start posting to build hype around your movie. However, be careful not to reveal anything from the set unless you coordinate and get approval from your distributors and publicity firms.

The still photographer will either be on set for the whole shoot, or if you are on a budget, you can pick and choose the most important days for them to arrive. It is considered a union job if your movie is a union film. The still photographer will have to be incredibly discreet and not interrupt the flow of the day or the shot. They cannot be in the "eyeline" of the actors, or end up accidentally in the shot. They need to have a very good eye for composition and grab the most intense moments so you'll be able to use them for publicity stills later.

Make sure the leading actors sign off on the photos they like so that you can use them for publicity, and they will all be already pre-approved

It's a Wrap

As filming winds down, the excitement can be overwhelming, but it is very important to wrap properly. You must return all equipment and strike (dismantle) all sets. You should keep the main wardrobe and props in case you need to reshoot some scenes later. The script supervisor and the heads of department will provide pictures and notes for continuity to the editor.

Emotional goodbyes and an all-night wrap party will usually ensue. Try not to do anything to embarrass yourself.

It's a wrap! Go to sleep for a week.

PART FIVE
POSTPRODUCTION

Reimaging the Movie

The Editing Room—It's a Sanctuary

Final Cut

Test Screening Questionnaire

Pickup Day

The Score

Music Supervisor

Storytelling Through Sound

Visual Effects

The Title Sequence

Telling a Story with Color

Postproduction Supervisor

Deliverables

Fin

Reimagining the Movie

Once you become a normal person again and can sleep at night without dreaming that you are late to set, postproduction is an extremely exciting period of making your movie. The major pressures of prep and filming are subsiding, and all the drama on set becomes a distant memory.

You begin by referring to what the editor has assembled and the reality of what you managed to "get in the can" sets in. A whole new world opens up as you recreate and reimagine your movie. Give yourself time to mourn disappointments and marvel at some moments you never realized came alive so vibrantly.

Usually on a low-budget feature, postproduction will take about eight months between editing, composing music, working on VFX, test screenings, mixing, coloring, titles, and reshoots.

The Editing Room—It's a Sanctuary

Editors are often the calmest, coolest, and most collected people you'll meet during the filmmaking process, and the editing room is the place where you can finally sit quietly and reimagine your movie into what it will eventually become. A great editor will be able to bring a fresh look and approach to your story, and the collaborative process of working with them as a director is fascinating and fertile.

The first assembly should take the editor about two to three weeks after wrap and will contain every single scene in the movie. It should include temporary music and sound effects to enhance the overall feel. After that assembly, the director will start working on their cut with the editor.

Coming to the editing room to watch the first assembly, for some directors, is nerve-racking. I know of some who even take a tranquilizer. I am always excited and can't wait to go in. I have a pretty good sense of what I have shot, and I edit it in my mind. But more than that, I trust the editor will surprise me and create magical moments.

Once the producer watches the director's cut, they share their notes and give constructive criticism. A note such as cut twenty minutes out of the movie does not help. It is infuriatingly vague. If you feel you want to cut any scene or shorten a sequence, say why and give specific suggestions.

Per the DGA, a director receives a minimum of ten weeks of editing to deliver their cut, and then the producer/s are welcome to come in and give their notes. For non-union movies, the number of weeks given to the director is up to negotiation.

Final Cut

In the editing room, major celebrations and intense arguments often unfold concerning huge structural decisions or mere frames. The final decision is usually a contractual matter, depending on who has the most negotiating power, be it the director, producer, or financier.

I've found it's most effective for directors to involve producers early in the editing process. This collaborative approach helps ensure that by the time the director's cut is ready, the producer is aligned with the decisions made, and everyone can agree on the "locked picture."

❀ *Prior to committing to direct* A Thousand Kisses Deep, *I faced a difficult choice; either retain final cut while giving up most of my directing fee or take a director's fee and relinquish final cut rights. I chose the latter, trusting in a collaborative final edit. And with two kids at home, I couldn't afford to go a year without earning hardly anything. I had a wonderful time working with the Editor, Humphrey Dixon, and I loved our cut. But the producer chose to re-edit the opening and the ending of the film, completely altering the story.*

In the script ending, Jodie Whittaker's character kidnaps herself as a baby from the maternity ward, saving her future self from a bleak destiny with destructive parents. This act encapsulated the film's theme of reconciling past, present, and future selves. Instead, the producer edited the film so that Jodie's character leaves the baby in the maternity ward, symbolizing making peace with her past and her deceased mother.

This drastic change was heartbreaking both for me and for the novel writers, Alex Kustanovich and Vadim Moldovan. Despite my disappointment, I chose not to remove my name from the movie because I was proud of the performances and of many of the scenes. The film went on to be nominated for a British Independent Spirit Award.

On Jungle, Director Greg McLean and I shared final cut rights with a third producer from Arclight Films being prepared to step in as a tiebreaker if necessary. We debated for days about whether to cut Yossi's hallucination scenes about meeting with his parents and uncle and about a lavish life with huge tables of food in a fancy hotel room, which we had spent three full days filming. We built all those locations, and now we were thinking that perhaps the hallucinations would take us away from the terrors that Yossi is experiencing being alone in the jungle. Greg was adamant that they should stay while I wasn't sure. It was the same debate Justin and I had during the development of the script, so we tried a cut with and a cut without, screened them, and finally agreed together to keep them in. Greg's instinct was right.

Test Screening Questionnaire

Once you have a cut you are reasonably happy with, it is wise to start having test screenings. Book a screening room and invite some friends who will tell you the brutal truth. As you progress with the cut and make changes, have more screenings and hand out questionnaires to gauge people's opinions.

Include questions like:

- Who is your favorite character and why?
- Were you bored and if so, when?
- Who is your least favorite character and why?
- Did you understand the plot or were you confused?
- Did you like the music?
- Would you recommend it to your friends?

You can hire companies to arrange the screenings. These companies will find an audience that fits the target demographic for the movie and can even have cameras installed during the screening to see if the viewers jump at a scary scene or laugh at a joke. They will book the theater, handle the questionnaire, and analyze the results.

And remember, if you receive the same note repeatedly, you should probably pay attention and consider changes. If the notes vary, you can then refer only to the ones you like.

Pickup Day

During the editing process and even while filming, the editor, director, and producer will compile a list of missing shots that will be needed for the final edit. Sometimes what is missing are establishing shots to give context of a city or neighborhood. These are easy enough to get. Other times, the missing shots will be crucial to telling the story, developing characters, or explaining things in the event of clarity issues. These could be full new scenes that, when added, will elevate the story. The challenge is often scheduling actors who have moved on to other projects, gathering all props, wardrobe, and rebuilding partial locations. So, when you wrap, you have to keep all elements until you lock picture.

❈ *On the movie* Stranger Than Fiction, *directed by super-talented Eric Bross, there was a scene where a dead body is being disposed of in a vat of boiling chemicals. The script called for the body to disappear into the vat, leaving no evidence. But during filming, the "body" slowly began to sink but never disappeared completely, part of it remaining afloat and visible.*

Caroline Ross, the editor, asked us to film another shot of the last part of the body disappearing in the tank. She felt that otherwise the audience would be misled into thinking the body might be found and the main characters caught. We had shot the movie in Salt Lake City several months earlier and were back in LA for postproduction. We did not have the tank, the "body," wardrobe, camera equipment or our crew. We told Caroline we couldn't get the shot, but she kept insisting that all we needed to do was fill a trash can with bubbly water, put a small bag into it, and pull it underwater with a rope. As we started test screening the movie, we realized Caroline was right, and we shot that one insert. That extra shot saved the scene.

Funnily enough, years later on Breakwater, *also edited by Caroline, we once again needed to show a body sinking. James Rowe, who is really clever writer, wanted to* stay subtle with Dermot Mulroney's transformation and wrote a scene where Dermot rents a small boat with a local fisherman who takes him to the marsh to look for the hidden shack. In the next scene, we see Dermot alone on the boat, the implication being he killed the fisherman. It worked great on the page; however, during the test screenings, we realized that the audience had not understood the fisherman was dead. We needed to make it clearer that Dermot killed him and that he was a major loose cannon and a danger.

We could not afford to film a whole "killing scene" and came up with the solution. On our pick-up day in LA we shot the scene in a heated pool designed for underwater filming. We filmed the "body", an actor, wrapped in a fishing net, sinking. This gave us all we needed. It involved an underwater crew and a special underwater camera operator with diving equipment, plus a lifeguard. If only it had been as simple as a trash bag and a water bucket. All of this was possible due to producer Matt Paul, whose company Loose Cannon Pictures arranged for the financing of the film, was very passionate about the project and was there to support the artistic vision of the director. He raised the extra funds needed for the pick-up day.

The Score

Music in movies can elevate the audience's experience to another transcendental level, enhancing the emotional experience.

Through the score, you can bring a complementary layer to the storytelling rather than simply reinforcing what the picture is showing. It can serve as a reflection of the internal world of the character, the mood of the scene and even the theme for the entire movie. You might want to try to say something else through the score, perhaps hint at something in the character's past through a specific instrument from a certain period or location. It's the final touch to the character's sculpture.

There are many ways to approach scoring. Often there are specific themes or chosen instruments for different characters, which would repeat throughout the movie in different variations, or different arrangement orchestration, which instead give different colors to the same melody. The score can signal love, evoke a thrill, or enhance a comedic moment. Sometimes silence is the best score. Don't feel you need to score every moment in the movie.

The music editor will take the score and all the source songs and lay them down on the soundtrack to fit each scene properly. Therefore, the composer should deliver the score with separate tracks for each instrument so it can be manipulated in the final sound mix if needed.

❊ *On Breakwater, James and the magnificent composer Roque Baños, worked tirelessly to find a theme for Dermot Mulroney's complex character, Ray. He presented himself as a friend, a mentor and protector to the young naive star of the movie, Darren Mann. Midway through the movie he is revealed as a vicious manipulator and a killer.*

The challenge was how to score the scenes with him in the first half without revealing the twist. However, the score also needed to artfully foreshadow the darkness. Roque and James sat at the piano for hours talking about Dermot's past and how he transformed to become a "villain." Note after note, interval after interval, different pitches combined at the piano until something suddenly clicked.

It was the simplest combination of notes. It seemed like it was always there, perhaps a bit too shy to show up. It spoke so clearly that they both jumped from their chairs. Ray's theme had been born! It was so perfect that it fit instantly everywhere. Roque used a variety of instruments ranging from a badass distorted guitar, a solo fiddle, and even a big romantic symphonic orchestra (recorded live in Budapest, Hungary) to show the range of emotions and contradictions.

In another scene in the movie, Darren Mann and Mena Suvari are making out just hours after Darren's character was released from jail. The scene was designed to be filmed in one shot. We licensed the song "Dance Hall Days" by Wang Chung to play in the background, which was fun and upbeat. When the scene takes a turn and becomes darker, the nuances of the performances were lost. So, in post, we created an artificial dolly move in, pushing the camera closer to the actors, and at the sound mix sessions, we cross faded from the song to a creepy score piece. Those two changes gave the scene a whole other ominous layer.

Music Supervisor

The music supervisor is the curator of song choices. They will come up with ideas for songs or other composed music that is available for licensing. The rights to famous songs are usually very expensive. The music supervisor might instead bring in new, young artists who are seeking exposure and will give you their songs for a smaller fee. Sometimes songs in the public domain may also work for your movie.

During the editing process, the editor and director will create a temp soundtrack and try out different songs and existing scores to see how music can enhance your movie. This will be the reference to work off of for both the composer and the music supervisor.

❀ *After trying many different songs for the movie Breakwater, we all fell in love with "Friend of the Devil" performed by Mumford and Sons. It had just fit right; and added so much to the final shot of the movie. However, no matter how much we tried, we could not bring it down to a price we could afford. Finally, James came up with another song, "February Seven" by the Avett Brothers and our music supervisor, Mike Turner, managed to work miracles. We paid about half the price of the Mumford and Sons song. And, as often happens, we were lucky and the song and lyrics were even better suited for the final beautiful, emotional shot of the movie.*

Storytelling through Sound

Arriving at the sound mix stage is a monumental moment and one of the final phases in making the movie. The room is dark with a big screen to watch the movie. In front of it is a huge panel with a sound mixing console, which will bring up an almost limitless number of channels simultaneously, including those for the music, sound effects, Foley, and dialogue/ADR.

The sound effects editing and final mix will enhance the viewing experience dramatically. A distinct sound effect can recall an emotion, hint at upcoming danger, intensify the danger during a car chase, or raise feelings of longing with the sound of leaves or rain. Half of the perception of a good fight scene comes through the hits created on the Foley stage, where someone is hitting a sack of rice. The sound designers and mixers are true artists, bringing another layer to the storytelling.

Through sound, you can scare people and make them jump out of their seats, get them emotionally involved by hearing someone's heartbeat, or foreshadow danger or catastrophe by hearing ambulances, police sirens, or a specific ominous sound created specifically for the movie every time the "monster" approaches.

The sound mixer will be the one who takes all the different sound channels and mixes them together, and sometimes, even suggests muting some elements or saving them for a later part of the scene.

Foley is also a really fun part of post-sound work. The studios will have a special room with various surfaces to recreate footsteps seen in the picture as well as various pots and pans, water buckets, a boxing pad, and an endless number of props to create specific sounds.

Walla Group (or Loop Group) is a group of actors performing all the background murmur in the different scenes. During filming, the set has to be quiet, and the extras mimic talking so that the dialogue can be recorded clean of other sounds. Then, in post, all that murmur that would normally come from a crowd in the audience or guests of the restaurant will be added.

ADR is also crucial as oftentimes some lines need to be rerecorded because of either sound interference or the director's wishes to have another read or performance. Added lines or voice-overs can also be recorded to explain the plot better or add another layer of understanding of the scene. So when you negotiate the actors' contracts, it is important to add availability for ADR days.

❀ *In Kill Me Later, Selma Blair's character has just had enough; everything is closing in on her. As she sits alone in her bank office, the sounds start to get distorted, loud, and crazy. Then all sound stops in one second, and she runs to the roof to kill herself. The sound work externalized and dramatized her inner feelings.*

Later in the movie, when Selma and Max Beesley escape together, over a beautiful shot of them running on stairs, Tal Berman and Renato Neto, who composed the score, decided to record live loud breathings, which they then edited and turned into a score and sound effects. It worked perfectly and enhanced the audience's illusion of intimacy with the characters as they hear their rhythmic breaths.

During the premix to the movie Breakwater, James Rowe, the director, wanted to enhance the "fighting" sounds for the final battle between the hero Darren Mann and the villain Dermot Mulroney. As the Foley team was away, Mixer James Parnel had Producer Matt Paul and James stick their heads into a bucket of water on the Foley stage and used a hydrophone (waterproof mic) to get the sounds of Ray and Dovey struggling with each other underwater.

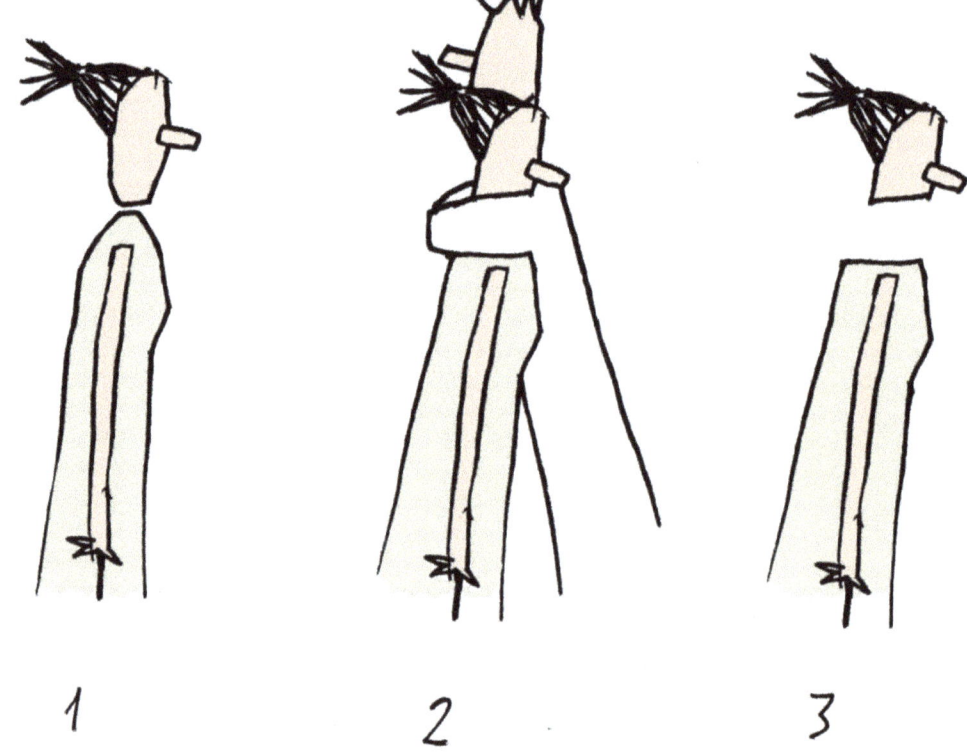

1   2   3

Visual Effects (VFX)

Visual effects are critical elements of almost every movie, and the possible uses of such effects are endless.

You should decide on VFX shots during the preproduction phase to properly budget them. You will then need to hire a VFX supervisor who will be on set when those scenes are filmed to make sure they are done in a way that will work for the VFX artists in post.

❀ *In the book version of Jungle, one of the most profound moments for me was when Yossi's feet were aching so badly that he could not walk. In order to survive, he had to reach the riverbank, which would be the only place where he could be spotted by a helicopter or boat. But he couldn't do it. He did not have the strength and stamina to keep walking. He knew he had to do something drastic and came up with an idea.*

He stood under a tree filled with fire ants that began to bite him mercilessly, and he shook the branches to have more of them land on his bare body. The excruciating pain of their bites was worse than the agony in his feet, and so with a new rush of adrenaline, he hobbled to the river to wash the ants off.

We weren't going to make Daniel Radcliffe endure thousands of fire ants, so the insects were created and added via VFX during post, but the red ants look completely real. We also spared Daniel from encountering a real tiger, which he scared away with a torch, creating one in post along with hundreds of colorful butterflies. The butterflies show Yossi embracing the beauty around him despite the harsh reality of being lost and in pain.

The Title Sequence

The front-title sequence, if executed well, can be exciting and creative and can quickly get the audience into the atmosphere of the movie and foreshadow what the movie is going to be like. Careful planning needs to occur to film the sequence, and it should be budgeted. But sometimes things change, new ideas sprout during filming and as with the whole process of filmmaking, you should embrace the unexpected inspirational idea.

❀ *As mentioned, while filming* Confessions of a Sociopathic Social Climber, *a tough, short seventeen-day shoot, I had an idea for a title sequence that was not written in the script. I imagined Jennifer Love Hewitt getting "dressed to kill," "arming" herself for the day, like any action movie hero. But instead of army shoes, knives, bullets, web belt and a vest, I saw Jennifer donning lipstick, stockings, high heels, a cigarette skirt and a strapless top. I talked with Jennifer about this, and she loved that idea.*

As an independent director and producer, I welcome new last-minute improvisational ideas, even if it means going out of my way to manifest them, but this was a network show, and the rules were more stringent. I naively approached someone in charge, excited to present my vision. However, they were adamant that we could not fit the scene into the schedule. When I insisted, they rudely and loudly dismissed me in front of the whole crew.

After they used a few obscenities, I decided to approach the producers. I presented my plan and they actually really liked it and approved. So I reworked the choreography for a talky exposition scene so we could film it in one shot and free up three hours. I asked for a clothes rack and a long zoom lens. We shot the whole scene from one angle using many sized snippet shots and lots of chaotic camera movement, music-video style. Jennifer shined and glowed performing her getting ready. The *only other expense was a designer bra Jennifer Love Hewitt requested. We now had a fun, energetic opening sequence for the price of a bra, a rack, and a zoom lens. The scene was used throughout the title sequence and, just as importantly, all over the trailer, which made sales of the movie skyrocket. The producers were ecstatic. And that person, oh well, I hope they have been treating the next indie female director, with more respect.*

Main and End Titles

It's a creative choice whether to have the main title sequence upfront at the beginning of the movie or leave it until the movie ends. Either way, it is important to follow the guilds rules and the contractual obligations. If the choice is to have the main titles at the end of the movie, there will still be the production companies' logos as well as the distributors at the opening.

For the end crawl, the post supervisor and the production coordinator will work on the long list of all cast, crew members and other contributors, based on customary orders and contracts. And there too, you can get creative by adding images, illustrations, or a font you established in the main titles. Accompanied by a great score or song, you might entice people to stay to watch the whole crawl.

Thank You Credits

Be generous here. If someone gave you good advice, agreed to read your script and gave you notes, came to a private test screening and then sat with you over lunch for two hours to talk about your movie, or they have been there for you, giving you warm soup and a shoulder after a challenging day on set, or any other help and support, give thanks. It only takes typing their name, and it can mean the world to them.

Telling a Story with Color

The color grading process is the final creative process in completing the movie. This process happens after the edit is locked and the sound mix is done. The movie is ready to be cut per the EDL (editing digital list) from the offline cut, using the highest resolution, original film footage.

Once the cut is done and all the VFX, CGI shots and titles are edited in, the color grading process will begin. The colorist will work with the director and cinematographer on a software in which they can go over each scene in the movie and make sure that the colors match from shot to shot, balancing them to give the movie a harmonized look.

Then the colorist will do a creative pass along with the director and DP. In that process, you can control the brightness and contrast, creating an atmosphere, lightening up the scenes, or making them gloomy. You can make the movie look more grainy or old, giving it all a sepia tone for a period look or a colder metallic feel for a sci-fi movie, for instance. You can also darken specific areas of a shot and brighten others to call attention to a specific detail. The LUT can serve as a first reference.

❀ *In Kill Me Later, the plan was to start the movie in greyish tones to give off gloomy feelings, and as the movie progresses and Selma Blair's character finds a will to live, the world becomes richer, brighter, and more colorful. However, when I got to the coloring sessions, I had just had my twins and I was nursing while working with the colorist, hardly able to stay awake. In hindsight, I should have pushed further for the original color concept and really gone for a more muted black and white look at the beginning. But my maternal joy got the better of me, and the movie doesn't reflect that much of a dramatic change colorwise. It looked great, but I still feel it was a missed opportunity to emphasize her arc from bleak to optimistic.*

Postproduction Supervisor

The post supervisor has a crucial role as they may deal with coordinating between the post-sound house, the editing room, the post color and grading and online facility, the title company, and the VFX artists. Beyond that, the post supervisor will help coordinate the finalized title role and upfront titles in the movie. This has to be done with the help of the production coordinator and lawyer as credits placements, and duration are all restricted by the contracts of the actors, heads of departments, and crew.

The post supervisor will coordinate the long list of deliverables needed to be delivered to the buyers and distributors around the world needed to sell the movie for both domestic and foreign markets and will prepare all the technical coordination for any festival submissions and exhibits.

The post supervisor will also help coordinate with the postproduction accountant in preparation for the final audit for all parties including the film commissions in the locations. Only after the submission of all accounting and the audit, will the tax rebates be received to pay back the bank loan or to be received by the investors.

Deliverables

When the movie has been completed and sold, the sales companies and distributors will have a long list of deliverables, which you will need to supply. For the foreign buyers, this includes extra materials, which will allow them to dub the movie to other languages in certain countries. It is important to be aware of this during production so you can prepare. It is a long list, but some of the main items are:

Technical Deliveries

- The DCP-Digital Cinema Package, which is basically the "print" of your movie. This is the final result.
- M&E track: A copy of the movie with only music and effects in the soundtrack without any dialogue so it can be dubbed to other languages in other countries.
- The final script with dialogue and continuity notes
- Main and end titles

Marketing Materials

- Key Art
- EPK (Electronic Press Kit) including behind-the-scenes materials
- Clearance of stills, which can be used for the poster and promos
- Trailer and poster if created
- Billing block (how credits are displayed)
- Film Festival Laurels—these are the symbols used to signify participation in a film festival or an award received from a specific festival.

Legal Documents

- E&O insurance
- Copyright registratio
- Title report showing the title of the movie is available
- Final chain of title
- Final waterfall
- All music clearances and signed contracts
- Cue sheet for residuals calculation of the song and music owners
- QC (quality control)—a technical check completed at the lab
- MPA rating of the movie

Fin

When everything is locked, you will receive a DCP, which is basically the "print" of your movie. And that's it. Just like that, your movie is done. All the hard work and hundreds of thousands or millions of dollars are saved on a small hard drive. It is kind of anticlimactic compared to the film days when we used to carry five eighty-pound reels of film in metal cans to film festivals. We would carry them on the plane so they wouldn't get lost or damaged. But then again, DCPs are more affordable, easy to ship around, and they are protected with a password in case they fall into the wrong hands.

And off you'll go. The next thing you know you'll be on your way to the screening!

The End!

PART SIX
The Film is Born

The Gods of Movies

Apply to Film Festivals

Attending Film Festivals

Producer's Representative

Domestic Distribution

In Theaters

Four Walling–Self Distribution

Key Art & The Poster

The Critics

The Gods of Movies

Finally, the movie is done! No going back. You have worked on this for years. You put your heart and soul into it. You may have even mortgaged your house (although I hope not). You have put a lot on the line to get your movie made, and now it's time to show it to the world and embrace whatever outcome.

You will submit to festivals and pray to get into the big ones, which could potentially change your career. But you will also submit to the not-so-acclaimed festivals in case you don't get into the top five, and I hope you'll allow yourself to celebrate those too.

If you can, arrange for a big, private premiere and invite the cast and crew as well as friends and family. You'll invite the distributors to come, and they may or may not, but I hope you'll celebrate that moment as well.

You'll try to find a foreign sales agent and when you do, you may choose to fly to the markets to see how the screenings go, to meet some of the buyers, to wine and dine at the big parties on the French Riviera and maybe watch other movies by other film makers, and again, celebrate. You did it; you are one of the few who had a dream, a concept and you completed it.

In the next few pages, I'll go through some of the main ways to have your movie exhibited out in the world. But just remember that sometimes, even if your movie is great and you did everything right, things beyond your control may effect the release, and that's okay. The gods of the movies have their ways, and you just need to trust that you have done your best and move to make your next movie.

Applying to Film Festivals

Attending film festivals is rewarding as you have the opportunity to finally exhibit your movie in front of film lovers who came to support filmmakers. If you're lucky, you'll fly to far-off places where you will be hosted and have your film celebrated. You'll sit on Q&A panels and talk about your process, the challenges you faced, and maybe even your dreams for your next project. You'll mingle with other filmmakers, form new friendships, and sometimes even find new partnerships. You will be anxious as you anticipate the first reviews. However, the festival is also a chance for you to sell the movie and to become eligible to submit the movie to awards competitions such as the Oscars.

Be sure to keep some funds in the budget to submit to festivals and to cover other expenses such as the costs of attending the festivals (like airfare and accommodations) if the festival won't cover them.

Knowing which festivals to submit your film to may be daunting. After all, hundreds of festivals are out there. Here are some tips:

- Make sure the festival is nonprofit, not a pay for play.
- Make sure they have been around for a while.
- Some festivals won't accept a film that has screened in another festival so you need to prioritize where to attend if you are accepted to a few.
- Check whether appearing at the festival will make you eligible for awards consideration (Oscars, guilds, etc.)

Attending Film Festivals

When accepted to a film festival, you'll need to prep. This is a great time to try and find a producer's representative who will attempt to sell the movie at the festival.

Hire a publicist who will help you make a splash and create buzz around the movie. It is best if your stars attend as well. Prep fantastic artwork and a teaser or trailer so the publicist can try to place your movie in the local press to entice people to show up at your screenings. You want a full room.

Have your next project ready to pitch, as you never know who you will meet. Maybe you'll be introduced to your next investor.

❀ *A movie I produced and was passionate about, The Frontier, was accepted to SXSW. We then started looking for a producer's rep to help us sell the movie at the festival. We hired a publicity firm, AMPRM, and strategized our attendance. To help promote the film, Director Oren Shai, created a forty-second teaser made of one shot extracted from the movie featuring beautiful Jocelin Donahue smoking a cigarette with shaky, bloody hands. Anne B. Kelly designed a stunning poster as well as post-cards featuring each character. The publicists were able to secure a couple of articles in the trades and the local news where they featured the poster and the teaser, and the movie started to gain some awareness at the festival.*

We invited our lead actors to attend the festival to walk the red carpet. We had a packed house for our screening and immediately after received two offers from domestic distribution companies. Oren was also approached by an agent to represent him. Bingo!

Producer's Representative

To sell your movie in the domestic market or in all of North America (i.e., the US and Canada), you can engage a producer's representative who will represent the movie and present it to the distributors. Most of the big talent agencies also represent movies. The producer rep serves as a sales agent, and they would first watch the movie and assess whether they think they can find a distributor and whether the movie can generate revenue before they will decide to take on your movie.

Producer reps usually charge ten percent of all revenues collected by the production company from the distribution of the film domestically. Some producer reps may charge an up-front fee and a commission for their service if they provide ongoing consulting services.

The producer rep will share the movie with domestic distributors and will negotiate the terms. If the movie plays in one of the big festivals such as Sundance or Toronto, they will promote the movie to the domestic buyers to have them attend the screenings. This would be the ideal time to sell a movie, after a hyped premiere at a festival with a full theater.

Domestic Distribution

When a domestic distribution company licenses a movie, the main terms that will be negotiated are as follows:

- **The Platform:** One of the most important elements in the distribution deal is on which platform the movie will be released. Will there be a theatrical release, or will it go straight to the different digital platforms. If the deal is for a theatrical release, it is important to define in how many theaters and in which markets/cities, it will be released and for how long.

- **P&A (prints and ads):** Relates to the theatrical release of the movie and defines how many "prints," i.e., in how many theaters the movie will be released and how much funds will be spent on the advertising and marketing of the movie in all available medias including TV ads, social media, posters around town, billboards, trailers, etc.

- **Minimum Guarantee ("MG" or "advance"):** If the movie seems to have real value in the market, the distributor may offer an upfront payment. This amount will be paid upon the delivery of the film. The MG will later be deducted from the producer's share of revenues.

- **The Term:** The agreed time of engagement, usually seven to twenty-five years, sometimes with an option to extend.

- **The Release Date:** The distributor will strategize and suggest the best time to release the movie, based on genre, target audience, holidays, other competing movies release dates and, the availability of theaters that could be booked.

- **The Distributor and Producer's Split of Revenue:** Here is a customary split:
  - First the domestic distributor will deduct their distribution fee, usually twenty to thirty-five percent.

- Then they will deduct their distribution expenses including the P&A.
- Then they will recoup their advance, if any.
- The rest is defined as "net revenues," which will be divided anywhere between one hundred percent to producer to a 50/50 split with the distributor.

The distributor and producer will work together to create all the elements needed for the release such as the poster and trailer. The PR firm may arrange for a "junket" where the lead actors and director will be interviewed back-to-back by as many publications and TV programs as possible.

In Theaters

Seeing your movie in the theater is the dream of every filmmaker. These days, however, it has become more challenging to successfully compete against studios and bigger indies for a big theatrical deal. Even independent theaters are now showing more mainstream movies. However, if you are lucky and the distributor sees potential for revenue and ticket sales, you might get a theatrical release.

Today, most theatrical releases for lower-budget indies are Day and Date, which means the film will be released concurrently in theaters and on VOD or SVOD. Another option is a short window, in which distributors will hold off from VOD release for two weeks to two months based on an evaluation of how long they think the film will play successfully in theaters.

The theatrical split between the theaters and the distributors will be where theaters take fifty to sixty percent, and the rest will be paid to the distributors. However, lower-budget indie movies will most likely receive less. This is because they are predicted to sell fewer tickets.

The first weekend in theaters is critical to the theatrical success of the movie, which can be predicted by the first weekend numbers. This is something which distributors pay close attention to before they commit to screening the movie for another week. They particularly watch to see whether there is a gain in attendance from Friday to Saturday because this indicates great word of mouth and a potential for a longer successful theatrical release. On the other hand, a drop in attendance most likely indicates that the movie will not perform well with an audience if it is extended.

❀ *For* Wedding Bell Blues, *we were offered a huge TV premiere deal. However, the network demanded the removal of two moments from the movie to fit the conservative audience. One was when Jasmine, the, edgy quirky character, played dazzlingly by Illiana Douglas, was filling her convertible with gas, and she told her friends she's slept with over a hundred men. Paulina, in a very serious manner, advised Julie Warner to masturbate after she admitted that she has never had an orgasm, all while a couple of shocked nuns were eavesdropping and giggling. The other moment was when Paulina's character was driven by her friends to have an abortion.*

The offer was tempting. It was a lot of money back then, and the exposure would have been huge. At the same time, we were offered a modest theatrical release for much less money, but nice P&A funds (prints and ads) guaranteed toward the publicity and release of the movie. The dilemma was tough. Remember, we did not make any money from the making of the movie, but ultimately, we chose to stay true to our vision and took the theatrical release offer! And when it came out, we were so excited that we drove from theater to theater to stand at the entrance and watch people buy tickets.

The competition, however, was tough. The First Wives Club was playing in theaters at the same time, so anyone looking to see a "date movie" was more likely to choose a big studio movie with huge stars. To combat our disadvantage, Ram and I stood by the marquis in different theaters, and as we saw couples debating what to see, we nonchalantly walked by them and mentioned that we had just seen and loved Wedding Bell Blues. We even printed some fliers and stood in front of theaters, handing them out to people. No one had any idea we were the filmmakers! And imagine how heartwarming it was when we overheard a young girl asking her mom what masturbation is as they were leaving the theater.

Would I have made the same decision today? I would probably choose the same path.

Four Walling—Self-Distribution

Four walling is a means of self-distributing your movie theatrically. If you cannot secure a domestic theatrical release, consider raising some funds to rent a theater, or a couple of them yourself, and exhibit the film. You would also want to hire publicity and invest in some ads, even if only on social media, to bring awareness and, most importantly, to get the movie reviewed. Even only one week in the theaters will qualify your movie to be submitted to the different awards competitions. When you pay the theater for the rental, all ticket sales revenue will be paid back to you and won't be split with the theater owners.

If you raise enough P&A funds, some indie domestic distribution companies can be hired to service a full domestic theatrical release for a fee.

❀ *The first movie we ever produced was called* Rave Review, *about a director in a small theater who accidentally kills a reviewer. Jeff Seymour, the writer, director, and star of the film who ran his own successful equity waiver theater, sent a letter to his subscribers asking if any of them were willing to invest in the movie…and they did! Many of Jeff's actor friends starred in the movie, including Ed Begley Jr., Marcy Lafferty Shatner, and Suzanne Wouk, who played Jeff's love interest.*

When the movie was done, Carole Curb distributed the movie in the foreign market through her company Curb Entertainment. However, we really wanted the movie in theaters in LA, so again we approached Jeff's subscribers. Through their generosity, we were able to four wall the movie. We rented the Laemmle Sunset Theater for a week and hired a PR company that managed to bring all the notable reviewers to the premiere. The LA Times gave the film a rave review, so we took out a couple of ads, and printed posters using quotes from their review, and off we went. We were on the map—legit filmmakers in the entertainment business!

Key Art and the Poster

The key art is the visual elements that will make the movie identifiable and unique. These elements will be used when designing the poster, any printed ads, social media ads, DVD covers, TV, cable or streaming ads, billboards, etc. Key art should be memorable so that people can instantly recognize the movie even without seeing the title.

Every element used in the creation of key art—from the picture chosen to fonts, background, colors, and the tagline—should tell the story of your movie! You can and should get very clever and inventive in the design. You can also add great quotations from good reviews on the poster and even a bad review may have a few pearls and words you could use. If you were accepted or attended a festival or won, make sure to add the graphic laurels and display it.

The billing block is the text that includes the names of the main actors, filmmakers, and production companies involved in making the movie. There are clear union/guild requirements regarding the order of credits in the billing block as well as contractually negotiated positions that must be honored. Some key art designers find creative ways to design the billing blocks while others maintain the traditional location of the block at the bottom of the poster.

❀ *For the* Jungle *poster, we chose a great image of Daniel Radcliffe looking up to the sky while standing in the river. To make it more poster-like, the graphic artist changed the background to a lush, green jungle, and we added a machete to Daniel's hand (with his approval, of course). We did something similar to the poster for* Breakwater. *The distributor insisted on adding a gun to Dermot's hand (with his approval), especially for the thumbnail, (the little image posted on the different platforms) to tempt you to click on it and watch the movie.*

The Critics

"There's only one thing in the world worse than being talked about, and that's not being talked about."—**Oscar Wilde**

We all crave a standing ovation from critics, desperately seeking good reviews and the Tomatometer's "Fresh" badge. Yet as we await the verdict of the critics, we are anxious. Critics can have enormous power over the success of a film, but their opinions should be taken and put in perspective. You can often read totally different reviews of the same movie. Remember, this is just one person's opinion; stand proud behind your work.

❀ *While getting ready for the release of Wedding Bell Blues, I flew to NY for some press engagements with Paulina Porizkova. There we went to dinner with her late husband, famed Cars front man Ric Ocasek, who very generously granted us the rights to use "My Best Friend's Girl" in the movie and trailer.*

Ric asked me in a protective way if I was ready for reviews. When I said that I hadn't thought about it until that moment, he told me that from his experience, when you see reviews printed in black and white, you somehow perceive them as absolute truth. If you get a stellar review, you feel like the king (or queen) of the world. But when you get a bad notice, you forget previous praise and are in danger of sinking into a cycle of self-doubt, loathing, and shame. His advice: don't read them at all. But if you do, don't let it rain on your parade.

This was amazingly valuable advice as I waited at the newspaper stand at Laurel Canyon and Ventura at 5 a.m. on the day of the movie's theatrical release. While a few of the reviews were great, praising and recommending the movie, that didn't matter to me. "Wedding Bell Snooze" was splattered in huge letters on the New York Times review page. Dejected I went home. But as people started to wake up, I got many congratulatory calls. People didn't care about the review; they probably didn't even read it. But they had seen in the paper the big, beautiful picture of Paulina, Illeana Douglas, and Julie Warner smiling while sitting in a red convertible. In there eyes that was the win.

On the other hand, receiving from Kevin Thomas of the LA Times, a quote such as "a gem." From the Hollywood Reporter, "You can practically hear the sighs of the women in the audience who relate to the problems of the three heroines," and "Lustig creates the kind of films the world could use more of." And to learn that your movie is included in Leonard Maltin's prestigious list of "50 movies that got away, movies you really ought to see," gives you the courage to continue and work on the next one.

"We must do our work for its own sake, not for fortune or attention or applause."
—Steven Pressfield, The War of Art

PART SEVEN
Encore

A Thought about AI

The Elegant Diamond Dealer on the Street Corner

It's not a Career; It's a Lifestyle

Acknowledgments

A Thought about AI

The technology is nothing without you. It is a powerful tool, but you are the person driving it." —**Walter Woodman**, *Shy Kids*

We are in the midst of a shift, a transformation the world has not experienced since the Industrial Revolution and the internet, and it's up to us to equip ourselves with digital literacy while different forms of AI emerge and evolve. I make an effort to educate myself, experiment, and learn to use new platforms, in order to develop, express, and conceptualize my individual vision.

I also enjoy watching content created by talented artists using AI technology. It's exciting to see how some videos are incredibly creative and fun. Ultimately, I don't mind if artists use AI, as long as their unique vision shines through in the context of their work. After all, nearly everything we watch is digitized and ultimately ends up in binary language—just ones and zeros.

We will all likely need to adapt and acquire new skills. Technological literacy is becoming a basic requirement and those who want to remain relevant to the industry will benefit from staying updated constantly on technological advancements.

It's clear that AI is much more than just a technology that can make everyone's life easier. It is a technology that can fundamentally change part of the industry beyond recognition. We tend to compare anything new to what we already know. However, with AI technology, we may see an entirely new industry emerge, bringing new kinds of storytelling tools that will be consumed differently—something that can't be compared to anything we have experienced thus far. For example, a story could be "written" in real time to match our specific preferences as we watch it.

In the near future, AI, might be able to receive and process our reactions and be able to analyze our physical state—such as our heart rate, our pupil movements, and even brain waves—in order to advance and customize the experience to the consumer. For instance, if we watch a movie and AI recognizes we are falling asleep, it may insert a huge explosion to the scene to wake us up. However, all of this can happen in parallel and in addition to the way we consume movies and TV shows today.

Storytelling has survived hundreds of thousands of years in different shapes and forms, and this is the time in history that society will consume stories that were not invented by humans. However, while none of the "creations" of AI can be considered art, it can be considered entertainment. Machines cannot create art as art is not a product. Art, in one way or another, expresses subjectivity which machines cannot have. AI produces images, clips, and stories out of very sophisticated, statistical mechanisms and algorithms. The machine can imitate human experiences, but it does not experience anything, so it cannot express new original insights about human existence and the world. The machine does not have the urge and need to share insights. It can only process, cultivate and adapt existing knowledge and create derivatives of it.

"In the endless stream of content, it requires a human "curator" to rescue meaning from the chaos."—**Jonathan Otcasek**

Throughout history, technology and art have been inextricably linked; so as creators, AI can give us new tools to do things that were not possible before, and make them more efficient and accessible. It can democratize filmmaking tools and help artists manifest their vision. AI has already been used for many years to help with so-called "busy work" and workflow, and frees us to focus on our creation. The technology could act as a collaborator of a sort, helping, for instance, to assemble sizzle reels, storyboards, decks, and iterate and present our vision for potential projects.

As to jobs in the film industry, many positions may be compromised; some already are as AI capabilities are being used, especially in the organizational fields, postproduction, visual effects, music, and more. However, new jobs are being created, and production companies are already seeking anyone at the forefront of the technology. AI may create lots of shortcuts and save us time, which we could use to be more creative and productive, but AI will never act, draw, write, or direct with a heart and soul or with nuance and subtext, along with a special quirkiness as only true artists can.

With all that said, strictly enforced measures are necessary when using AI in all areas of life to keep our world safe and thriving. Professional unions are successfully advocating for these evolving rules. One crucial aspect is ensuring that AI is clearly identified as such. To protect the integrity of creative fields, we must establish ethical guidelines and mechanisms to prevent AI from replacing human artists and undermining artistic authenticity. Significant strides have been made in regulating AI in the arts, particularly regarding the replacement of actors and writers. However, it's important to monitor ongoing developments, as this field is evolving rapidly.

In light of all that is going on, I do see a trend of artists coming together to form creative communities, to meet, interact, and talk with each other. And so, we stand a real chance that AI will stay a tool rather than become the downfall of artists.

The Elegant Diamond Dealer on the Street Corner

My smart, charming, and beautiful grandmother, who spoke five languages, was a single mother and had to find a way to support her mother and her daughter. She decided to become a diamond dealer. However, back in the late forties, women were not allowed into the diamond exchange buildings in both New York and Antwerp, Belgium, where she moved after WWII. But my grandma was determined.

She stood alone on the street corner across from the bourse (the diamond trade center) and started dealing diamonds on her own. In a short time, everyone got to know the elegant, sharp, and reliable woman with an excellent quality of certified diamonds at the street corner.

Customers would close deals with her based on a handshake, saying, "Mazel and bruche" (luck and blessing in Yiddish). Years later, when my grandmother was telling me the story over a hot matzah ball soup, there was never a sense of anger, frustration, or feeling inferior. This was the situation; she didn't argue with reality. She just plunged in and did what she was set to do, and I admired her for that.

Lots of things have changed since then, and women have broken the glass ceiling in incredible ways, including in the film business. I applaud all those who have bravely stepped up and shared their experiences leading to major changes in the industry and in people's minds. I notice a significant increase in the diversity of gender, race, and ethnicity represented in directors, cinematographers, writers, cast, and all other crew positions, creating a much more balanced community.

Yet people still ask me how it is to be a female filmmaker. I honestly reply that mostly, I don't think about it. I was, and still am, busy planning, developing new projects, and finding great stories to tell, always moving, trying to "do the work."

When someone asks me where I'm from, I am surprised. Oh, yeah, it's the accent. I don't think about the fact that I have one, or that I am a female, or a foreigner, or Jewish, in any context other than when it applies to the content of the project I'm involved with.

The movies I've directed have all featured female protagonists, not because of any agenda but because it feels natural for me. Those have been the stories I was passionate to tell, many of them derived from my experiences, and I relate to them on a personal level. I directed *Kill Me Later* while five months pregnant with my twins, and I nursed them in studios around town during postproduction.

When they were three years old, I rented a house on Victoria Island where I was directing *Confessions of a Sociopathic Social Climber*, hoping the twins would stay with me and I'd be a super mom, directing and mothering. Half an hour into their visit, I canceled the lease and told the nanny and my husband that they would need to take the kids back to LA. I realized I couldn't do both, and at that point in time, I was committed to my directing job, which had to come first.

A few days later they flew away. I wiped my tears and moved to a hotel, called the local hairdresser who came to my room every few days to blowout my hair. I showed up well-rested, collected, and ready to work.

I take responsibility for my life and career despite the different challenges that may come along by being a woman. On some occasions, I was advised to behave in more of a "manly manner," not to wear my feelings on my sleeve, be tough, and other "this or that" advice. But here is the thing; I have learned that every time I try to behave like someone else, it comes back to bite me. And I learned that the only way I can really operate is being me, with my quirky manner, my accent, my fast talk, getting to a point sometimes in a roundabout way, through a story or an anecdote, and with yes, lots of energy, enthusiasm, sometimes naivete and lots of emotions. It's just me. I feel that my work is a wonderful opportunity to use the limitations as a departure point, and if I'm honest and brave about it, I can turn them into my unique voice and an advantage.

At the end, I strive to be judged solely by the work I do and try to come up with interesting projects to spread positivity and love. I embrace my failures and successes, and it's up to me to get up every morning and continue on my path.

It's not a Career; It's a Lifestyle

I live and breathe movies. On any gloomy day, as bad as it might be, my religion, escape, inspiration, companion, guide, and mentor is watching a great movie or a TV show. I am grateful that I was blessed with that love and passion that gives me my compass in life. I think about stories for movies all day long. Almost any situation during my day can spark an idea, which might sound like an obsession, but this is how my brain works. It's part of who I am. However, both creatively and practically, it is a demanding and unpredictable lifestyle.

As a filmmaker married to a drummer, our schedules revolve around our careers. When our friends plan their summer vacation months in advance, we wait until the last minute; "the gig" comes first, and we never know when and where it will lead us. You might need to take phone calls in the middle of family dinners, while driving kids to school, or even on a boat ride in the middle of Lake Como during a family vacation, but it's the call of duty. I left home for months and traveled to make movies in distant locations such as England, Canada, Australia, Colombia, and Europe. It is tough to leave the family, but it's also a great adventure. I have chosen this path as a lifetime mission, and I can't wait to see where the next journey will take me.

But also creatively, "it" follows me all day long. Sometimes when I drive, do dishes, run on the treadmill, take out the garbage, or just wake up in the early morning to have my first coffee, and my husband or my kids try to speak with me, I stop them and tell them I'm working ... because oftentimes the best ideas come in those moments when my mind is free of all distractions and is purely available to be original and creative.

For the script *Tent*, about a young, troubled kid who runs away from home to join a traveling carnival, something was missing and I couldn't figure out what it was.

This drove me crazy for weeks. Then, one day, I was swimming, and as I was diving deep, I stayed underwater for a bit. Suddenly it came to me, the Eureka moment! I swam up and screamed, "I got it!" I realized we had to "revive" the kid's dead father so that his reason to run away from home would be to reunite with his estranged dad. This example is only to say how much our lives and our art are always intertwined.

One of the hardest things in this business is not knowing when the next job is coming. You always kind of fear that you may never make another movie. Some days I get so worried I think about alternatives. I have planned to import organic diapers and tampons, become a realtor, a hairdresser, or a midwife. But a day or two into my new venture, I realized I couldn't. I love movies. It's my calling, and I am willing to bear the insecurities and the challenging times, as I can't really do anything else with all my heart. So take this, as a time to nurture new ideas. Practice your art and craft, write, read, and keep learning. I might take an acting class, perhaps a writing seminar. I go to museums, travel, meet new people, reunite with my friends, listen to master classes, podcasts and lots of music, all to keep my creative mindset and, of course, watch many movies and TV shows.

They always say it's about who you know. So get to know people. I arrived in LA not knowing anyone in the business. But going to film school, working on set with other people who were just starting, forming friendships and partnerships, and growing in the industry together with my peers, has actually been the best entry for me.

And talking about connections, when you are up, when you are working and in a position to help, do it. Support a young filmmaker or an older filmmaker who hasn't been working for a while but has so much knowledge and experience; give them a chance again. It can be a cruel business, and you never know what a call for a job could mean for someone. It could mean the world to them.

In the movie *Rave Review*, the moral conclusion and last line in the movie was "there are no shortcuts."

Throughout the years, this line has resonated loudly. It takes a lot of hard work to become a filmmaker, and just as much to stay one over the years. I think anyone who starts in this business comes with passion and dreams and a great urge to tell stories and somehow inspire other people. Most don't get into it for the money. If you don't give up, and no job is below you—whether you sit on the director's chair with your name printed on the back or around the extras table—if you believe in your project and keep it vibrant, it might happen.

It took me twelve years to bring *Jungle* to the screen. My friends, my family, and some people in the industry, all told me to give up on it, to stop spending so much time and energy. Some projects are not meant to happen. It took a lot out of me not to listen and to continue my efforts, and it worked out. So when I feel like giving up, like a certain project isn't happening and everyone around me is tired of hearing about it, I remind myself that it's up to me to keep it "alive" and give it another chance until I finally make it.

You have to put in serious, tedious work to make a film, and there are lots of ups and downs. I have had great success with the movies I have directed and/or produced, but I also have a drawer full of scripts and ideas for movies that haven't been made yet. Still, I feel as enthusiastic about making movies today as I did back when I started. And though there are incredible highs and some very low moments, I hope to make movies until the end of my time. I have partnered and collaborated with many amazing, talented people. I direct, produce, and executive produce movies and TV shows, and as a way of giving back, I enjoy lecturing and mentoring new filmmakers. Film is my profession and my hobby. I hope what I've learned will help you on your journey in this business so you too can take the plunge and create movies you will love...and hopefully other people will too!

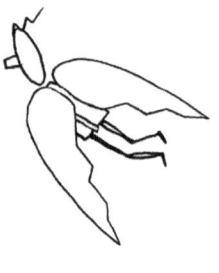

When you find yourself at home, lost in shadows of doubt, wondering if you will ever make another movie, while friends share smiles from movie sets and red carpets at film festivals, remember the reason you began this journey:

The love for movies, the passion for storytelling.

Return to the drawing board.

Let your inspiration flow onto the page, and dream of your next project.

Acknowledgments

Ok, colleagues, friends and family, the book is done and so I won't nudge you again asking you to review and comment. But for the times I did, here are my humble thanks

To **Diana Wilburn**, a designer with impeccable taste, you brought your magical touch to artistically and cleverly design the book and the cover and even changed its title. You took the book from design to print. I am lucky beyond belief you entered my life. I am eternally grateful.

My deepest gratitude to **Ben Reder**, my entertainment lawyer, for your careful review of the book and professional insights. I'm privileged to be your client.

To **Annette Goliti Gutierrez**, my longtime screen-writing collaborator and close friend, thank you for jumping on the wagon to edit the book and I can't wait to lure you into our next project. Special thanks to **Samantha Silvay**, the fastest script and book reader and editor I know. It's so much fun working with you.

To **Dan Mackler**, senior vice president/dean of New York Film Academy LA, thank you for your insightful notes, and for igniting this whole thing by inviting me to lecture.

Gadi Wildstrom, partner/Co-CEO of Freeway Entertainment, **Adam Taylor**, President/CEM of APM Music, **Clay Epstein**, president and founder of Film Mode Entertainment, **Glen Reynolds** of Circus Roadshow, **Peter Jarowey**, Co-CEO of Vertical Entertainment, **Kent Hamilton** President of Front Row Insurance Brokers, Postproduction Supervisor **Jeff Maynard** and **Einat Penarski**, lawyer at AHO law Tel Aviv, I thank each of you for years of collaboration and invaluable insights for the book.

To **Steven Pressfield**, the brilliant author and screenwriter, you encouraged me to Put My Ass Where My Heart Wanted to Be. Thank you. Your writing makes me laugh and cry, but your warm heart and belief in me give me the courage to wear my boots and *Do The Work.*

To my friend, innovative, gifted artist, **Yasmine Amitai-Murro**—thank you for your wisdom, smart, intuitive and candid advice. I am incredibly touched by your support and encouragement.

My dear friend **Michal Biel**, a spiritual mentor and author, thank you for always being there with support and advice.

Thank you, my friend, **Suzanne Wouk**, actress, writer, and tech entrepreneur, for reminding me to stay authentic and helping me focus my message.

Gregory Bernstein, author, great screenwriter, and friend, thank you for your enlightening notes and direction. **Alex Kustanovich**, thanks for your prompt notes and humor. Author **Ira Miller** and producer **Matt Paul**, you were one of the first to read the book; your validation meant a lot. **Eduardo Russoff**, thank you for letting me kvetch and giving me good advice. **Yarin Lidor**, I truly appreciate your help.

To **Yuval Robichek**, whose illustrations inspired me while writing the book—your depictions of love, heartbreak, and hope, all with a wink, were a catalyst for many ideas in the book. I'm grateful to you for allowing me to include your artwork.

In memory of **Bill Immerman,** my wonderful lawyer for many years, your wisdom, knowledge, incredible stories, and sense of humor are truly missed.

And to my family, **Tal**, **Maya**, and **Guy**, you are my everything. I would be in a remote Ashram looking for answers without you.

READY TO TAKE THE PLUNGE?

www.ingramcontent.com/pod-product-compliance
Lightning Source LLC
Chambersburg PA
CBHW042357030426
42337CB00030B/5131